Gender and Sexuality in Israeli Graphic Novels

This book explores how Israeli graphic novelists present depictions of masculinity and femininity that differ from conventional portrayals of gender in Israeli society, rejecting the ways that hypermasculinity and docile femininity have come to be associated with men and women.

The book is the first to explore Israeli graphic novels through the lens of gender. It argues that breaking down existing gender delineations with regards to masculinity and femininity is a core feature of the Israeli graphic novel and comics tradition and that through their works, the authors and artists use their platforms to present a freer and looser conceptualization of gender for Israeli society. Undertaking close readings of Israeli graphic novels that have been published in English and/or Hebrew in the last 20 years, the book's texts include Rutu Modan's *Exit Wounds* and *The Property*, Ari Folman and David Polonsky's *Waltz with Bashir*, Galit and Gilad Seliktar's *Farm 54*, and Asaf Hanuka's "The Realist".

This book will be of interest to students and scholars in comics studies, Israel Studies, Jewish Studies, and Gender Studies.

Matt Reingold is a member of the Jewish History and Jewish Thought departments at TanenbaumCHAT in Toronto, Canada. He earned his PhD from York University, Canada, and his doctoral research focused on the intersection between arts-based learning and Jewish Education. He has published articles on Jewish and Israeli graphic novels, Israel education, and arts-based Jewish education.

Routledge Focus on Gender, Sexuality, and Comics
Series Editor: Frederik Byrn Køhlert, University of
East Anglia

Routledge Focus on Gender, Sexuality, and Comics publishes original short-form research in the areas of gender and sexuality studies as they relate to comics cultures past and present. Topics in the series cover printed as well as digital media, mainstream and alternative comics industries, transmedia adaptions, comics consumption, and various comics-associated cultural fields and forms of expression. Gendered and sexual identities are considered as intersectional and always in conversation with issues concerning race, ethnicity, ability, class, age, nationality, and religion.

Books in the series are between 25,000 and 45,000 words and can be single-authored, co-authored, or edited collections. For longer works, the companion series "Routledge Studies in Gender, Sexuality, and Comics" publishes full-length books between 60,000 to 90,000 words.

Series editor Frederik Byrn Køhlert is a lecturer in American Studies at the University of East Anglia, where he is also the coordinator of the Master of Arts program in Comics Studies. In addition to several journal articles and book chapters on comics, he is the author of *Serial Selves: Identity and Representation in Autobiographical Comics*.

Cosplayers
Gender and Identity
A. Luxx Mishou

Gender and Sexuality in Israeli Graphic Novels
Matt Reingold

Infertility Comics and Graphic Medicine
Chinmay Murali and Sathyaraj Venkatesan

https://www.routledge.com/Routledge-Focus-on-Gender-Sexuality-and-Comics-Studies/book-series/FGSC

Gender and Sexuality in Israeli Graphic Novels

Matt Reingold

Routledge
Taylor & Francis Group

LONDON AND NEW YORK

First published 2022
by Routledge
2 Park Square, Milton Park, Abingdon, Oxon OX14 4RN

and by Routledge
605 Third Avenue, New York, NY 10158

Routledge is an imprint of the Taylor & Francis Group, an informa business

© 2022 Matt Reingold

The right of Matt Reingold to be identified as author of this work has been asserted by him in accordance with sections 77 and 78 of the Copyright, Designs and Patents Act 1988.

British Library Cataloguing-in-Publication Data
A catalogue record for this book is available from the British Library

Library of Congress Cataloging-in-Publication Data
Names: Reingold, Matt, author.
Title: Gender and sexuality in Israeli graphic novels / Matt Reingold.
Other titles: Routledge focus on gender, sexuality, and comics.
Description: Abingdon, Oxon ; New York, NY : Routledge, 2021. |
Series: Routledge focus on gender, sexuality, and comics |
Includes bibliographical references and index.
Identifiers: LCCN 2021012788 | ISBN 9780367713515 (hardback) |
ISBN 9780367713522 (paperback) | ISBN 9781003150435 (ebook) |
ISBN 9781000437188 (adobe pdf) | ISBN 9781000437256 (epub)
Subjects: LCSH: Graphic novels–Israel–History and criticism. |
Gender identity in literature. | Sex role in literature. | Sex in literature.
Classification: LCC PN6790.I7 R45 2021 | DDC 741.5/95694–dc23
LC record available at https://lccn.loc.gov/2021012788

ISBN: 978-0-367-71351-5 (hbk)
ISBN: 978-0-367-71352-2 (pbk)
ISBN: 978-1-003-15043-5 (ebk)

DOI: 10.4324/9781003150435

Typeset in Times New Roman
by Newgen Publishing UK

For Sloan and Nora, the next generation of graphic novel readers

Contents

Figures

Acknowledgements

Having written this book primarily during a global pandemic and economic shutdown, I feel incredibly fortunate to have actually had time to write this manuscript. If not for my children's daycare making heroic and herculean efforts not only to reopen, but to do so in a way that was safe for the children to return while still providing a nurturing and fun environment, this book would never have been written.

The origin story for this book can be traced to a childhood steeped in Marvel superheroes, Ninja Turtles, and Mighty Morphin' Power Rangers, and I thank my parents for indulging these interests. I am particularly appreciative of how my mom nurtured a love of reading and a commitment to Jewish education, and how she was a role model for curiosity and learning. I am equally grateful to Darryl Spires at Cyber City Comix for always being willing to put my weekly pulls on hold and for answering my annoying calls about whether anything new is in for me.

When I began my Master of Education degree at York University in September 2008, I had no idea such a thing as comics studies existed. Neither did my first instructor Neita Israelite. On the first day of Disability in Society, Neita provided us with the latitude to choose our own research topics, and I asked her if I could write about how the blind superhero Daredevil operates within Marvel's superhero universe. Despite not knowing anything about superheroes, comics, or me, Neita was curious enough to see where it would take me. Looking back, that conversation was a seminal moment in my life, as it led me on the path that I now walk; Neita's commitment to putting her students' interests first and foremost shape the way that I approach my own learning and teaching, and I am forever grateful to her.

A brief foray into disability studies through comics would lead me to discover comics studies and my own subfield of Jewish comics studies.

Josh Lambert's willingness to supervise a directed reading course for me on Jewish graphic novels even though I was not registered at his university introduced me to texts and topics that I did not know about, and his early encouragement led to my first publications on Jewish graphic novels.

The field of Jewish comics scholars is not so large, and I have benefitted tremendously from the work of others. While I do not know most of you in person, your work and infrequent online conversations have influenced my own and been formative in helping me develop my own understandings of Jewish graphic novels. These scholars include Victoria Aarons, Samantha Baskind, Assaf Gamzou, Rachel S. Harris, Tahneer Oksman, Ranen Omer-Sherman, and the late Derek Parker Royal.

Frederik Byrn Køhlert has been a wonderful guide through the publishing process, believing in the project and helping to see the book develop from an idea into the text that you are now holding. I am equally appreciative of Routledge for the care and attention that they have given to the manuscript and to the anonymous reviewers whose feedback enhanced the work. Any errors that remain are solely mine.

I have also had the great fortune to benefit from many wonderful institutions which have supported me over the years. These include the Wexner Foundation, where I was a Davidson Scholar, and York University, where I serve as a research associate at the Centre for Jewish Studies. The opportunity to receive funding, mentorship, and library access was invaluable. For the last 12 years, TanenbaumCHAT has been my home away from home. I am very appreciative of my colleagues, especially those in the Jewish History department, for their support over the years, and of Eli Mandel for his encouragement of my research and writing. I also want to thank Alexandria Silver for her thoughtful comments on a draft of the manuscript.

Finally, I am forever grateful to my loving and nurturing family, especially to my brother Ben and his wife Jess (who read chapters days before giving birth). My mom has been my co-biggest fan, and having her cheer me on always made a difference. And most importantly, I am grateful to my wife Chani, whose combination of encouragement and critical inquiry have improved not only this book, but also my life.

This book is dedicated to my daughters Sloan and Nora, future comic book readers and Zionists. My hope for them is that Israel will continue to evolve and become an even more inclusive, diverse, and integrated society, one that reflects the visions of many of the authors and artists included in this book.

Portions of Chapter 2 were first published in *The Journal of War & Culture Studies* and *Shofar* and portions of Chapter 3 were first published in *The Journal of War & Culture Studies, The Journal of Holocaust Studies*, and *Shofar*. I am grateful to the editors for allowing me to use revised versions of these articles in this book.

Introduction

Matt Reingold

Like every other country in the world, 2020 was a highly challenging year for Israel. A strong early response led to success against COVID-19 that garnered the small Middle Eastern country international accolades,[1] allowing it to serve as a model for Western countries that were not yet affected by coronavirus. But this same strong response also led to widespread economic shutdowns across the country and increased dependence on government financial assistance, as the country headed towards economic collapse.[2]

Unwilling to heed the recommendations of their elected officials, Israelis began actively staging protests and counter-protests in support of and in opposition to Prime Minister Benjamin Netanyahu and his government's policies.[3] During the spring and summer of 2020, two individuals came to characterize the plight of the average Israeli citizen who is suffering under the burdens of coronavirus and a government that is increasingly being accused of indifference to the public's experiences. The first is falafel seller Yuval Carmi. Faced with the prospect of losing his business because of restrictions preventing restaurants from serving food, Carmi delivered an impassioned plea to Netanyahu and his government to help struggling businesses, weeping as he revealed that he was almost US$20,000 in debt and considering suicide.[4] The second is an anonymous social work student whose actions went viral after she bared her breasts while atop the national symbol of the menorah at a rally. Protesting against the low wages and high hours that are expected of social workers, she explained that baring her breasts was not initially planned as part of her protest but "it is absurd that a woman's breasts can make such huge headlines ... even while the country is on fire and there are more than a million unemployed" as the substance of her protest became overshadowed by her methods.[5]

DOI: 10.4324/9781003150435-1

While there were some who vocally supported the two, both Carmi and the social work student experienced negative feedback from members of Israeli society. Carmi was accused of being an opportunist and of not even being poor, with incorrect claims appearing in the media that he had multiple yachts in Israeli harbors.[6] Carmi was so affected by the negativity that he required hospitalization for a heart procedure, but even when he was hospitalized, a man recognized him and called him a crybaby, claiming that he, too, had gone bankrupt but did not cry on television like Carmi did.[7] Similarly, the menorah protestor was castigated by numerous politicians for what they saw as a desecration of sacred national symbols. Prominent politician Yariv Levin announced that the woman needs to be "brought to justice, not just to punish her, but also for the educational and civic message that needs to be very clear".[8] Tali Ploskov, a parliamentarian in Netanyahu's ruling Likud party, commented on Twitter: "Not like this. Protest is a right, sometimes even a must, but not like that. Not in undressing, not in violence, not in bestiality. Not by humiliating the state emblem. You exaggerated; you lost your way. I would listen to you, but not like that".[9]

Choosing to start this book by examining recent Israeli protests might be a curious way to begin a book about gender in Israeli graphic novels. Yet what unites them is Israeli society's gendered response to the ways that Carmi and the social worker protested. For his willingness to reveal his feelings and to cry in public, Carmi was emasculated and considered to have behaved dishonorably. Similarly, permitting the social work student's right to protest but rejecting her use of her body as the conduit for her protest projects a normative gendered construct onto her body which is at odds with how she has chosen to present her protest. What both the menorah protester and Carmi experienced was the imposition of notions of hegemonic masculinity and femininity on the way they comport themselves within Israeli society. With a fairly rigid tradition of gendered expectations of men and women, behaving in ways that run counter to the hegemony breeds opposition and rebuke within Israeli society. Throughout this book I return to the question of what it means to perform gender in Israeli society. I contend that Israeli graphic novels articulate a vision for Israeli society that is at odds with the ways that both Carmi and the social worker were received by the wider Israeli community.

The ways that gender is performed in the public and private spheres is a topic that is central to Israeli identity and is as relevant and contested in 2021 as it was when the state was founded in 1948. Rachel S. Harris has written extensively about how a series of national narratives was created in the early years of the state in order to reinforce particular ways of building the nascent nation.[10] These nation-building stories revolved around Jewish history, Jewish identity, Jewish language, and the role that the new country would play in redirecting the narrative of Jewish history from one of suffering under the yoke of foreign rule to one of triumph as an independent nation. Israeli national narratives were shaped, developed, disseminated, and protected by the government, popular culture, the media, and national institutions.[11] These narratives also involved the establishment of gendered archetypes or hegemonies that men and women were expected to conform to.

Jewish-Israeli gender norms, and masculine norms in particular, emerged out of a rejection of a stereotype of gendered positions that were adopted by European Jews. Daniel Boyarin has shown that despite Israeli perceptions that European-Jewish masculinity was weak and effeminate, when situated within the context of the European Jewish community, it was not perceived negatively by fellow Jews. In fact, "the gentleness of the rabbinic male can only be imagined as sexlessness, encoded as unattractiveness" because of a desire to reject the ways that he performed his gender as a Jewish male.[12] Boyarin argues that contemporary Jews who reject the rabbinic male on the grounds of his being not manly fail to recognize that he was not endemic to Europe and his gendered identity is actually a component of Jewish gender norms for over 1,000 years. Within his community he was revered for his scholarly erudition, kindness, and compassion. Jacob Neusser cites what he calls the "affective program of the Rabbis", wherein Jews were encouraged to practice "humility, generosity, self-abnegation" and to reject being self-centered, vengeful, and temperamental.[13]

Israeli Jews' rejection of a stereotypical construct of the European Jewish man's gendered identity was modeled on the ways that non-Jewish Europeans categorized the Jewish male as effeminate and therefore inferior.[14] By adopting the prevailing negative and anti-Semitic associations with Jews' bodies[15] and by viewing nineteenth and twentieth century Jews who lived under oppressive conditions in Europe as weak, feeble, impotent, and therefore feminine, Israelis crafted a gendered identity that strove to be diametrically opposite from their Jewish-European predecessors.[16] This new Jew would be a hypermasculine version of the stereotypical non-Jew who oppressed Jews; adopting this persona would allow Israeli Jews to become like those who dominated society and not like those who were subjugated in society.[17] The Israeli male would reject the exilic experience of the Jewish European and would seek "to transform the Jewish body itself, and especially the sexual body" through a sexual revolution that would produce strong and powerful Israelis.[18]

Within Israeli society, the ideal or hegemonic Jewish male came to be identified with the warrior, one who fights to ensure the survival of the state and one who protects the country against its enemies.[19] This man would be heterosexual,[20] manly, "bound to the soil",[21] "a fighter and a conqueror, physically competent, courageous and aggressive, virile and unemotional".[22] He should align his interests with the nation's interests and not pursue selfish ends.[23] Within Israel, hegemonic masculinity, which is defined as "the most valued and dominant form of idealized masculinity",[24] became synonymous with a form of hypermasculinity,[25] leading to exaggerated behaviors which would connote what it means to be a man.

Given the mandatory military conscription in Israel which begins at the age of 18 for Jewish males, the hegemonic masculine role is primarily expressed through the valorization of soldiers. Raz Yosef argues that in Israeli society, "war is ... an education in masculinity".[26] This education continues even after the conscription period concludes, because there follows a subsequent period of reserve duty which continues for approximately 20 years. These reservists, suggests Lior Sion and Eyal Ben-Ari, are considered the epitome of masculinity because of their willingness to remain in peak physical conditioning for the benefit of the state.[27] The army also helps govern Israeli masculinity by assigning classifications and ranks to men which serve to create hierarchies among Israeli men.[28] Crafting the ideal masculine body begins during a young male's high school years and requires a particular type of fitness program. Within Israeli society, steroid-assisted and overly muscular physiques are not reflective of hegemonic masculinity; instead, the desired body is both lean and muscular. Performing hegemonic masculinity is not merely being able to adopt a superficial and physical guise of masculinity. Gabriella Spector-Mersel has argued that demonstrating masculinity within the established norms of a society helps to form an individual's self-worth and self-confidence.[29] Historically, being in possession of these traits, suggests Yehuda Sharim, provides evidence for a man's ability to demonstrate that he is able to be a good Israeli citizen.[30]

David Biale identifies a significant tension in Zionist ideology given its interrelatedness with masculinity; so long as gender norms were primarily crafted around men, women would struggle to find a place of equality within Israeli society.[31] As a country, Israel is considered a developed, post-industrial nation with a high quality of life. The country has a high per capita income and high rates of literacy and education. Concurrent with its high standard of living is the fact that Israeli society places tremendous emphasis on the nuclear family, and Israelis have among the highest fertility rates among OECD countries. The high fertility rates and concomitant postpartum expectations on women have led to a "strongly gendered society in which women have yet to achieve equality in almost all social domains".[32] Orna Blumen and Sharon Halevi write: "Conventionally, Israeli men assume the political and military preservation of the nation, and women care for its biological and social reproduction".[33] They note that despite claims to the contrary, or that men and women serve different yet equal roles, statements that suggest equality between the two genders in Israeli society are a myth. These different roles were established in the earliest years of the state, when men were assigned 'masculine' roles like farming the land and women were responsible for 'feminine' tasks like cooking and cleaning when both genders worked on *kibbutzim*, state-supported agricultural settlements.[34] Tami Amanda Jacoby extensively documented how despite *seeming* to have equal access in Israeli society, given equality's inclusion in the country's Declaration of Independence and the conscription of women into the army, "the reality of gender equality in Israel is that women are relegated to the margins of civic structures as a result of entrenched institutionalized and cultural forms of patriarchal authority".[35]

In contrast to the hegemonic man, the hegemonic woman in Israel primarily serves as an emotional support to the men in her life; she is someone in need of protection and who worries over the soldiers who have gone out to fight. Permitting the differentiation of gender roles, suggests Michal Frenkel, is tied to an existential fear that if high birthrates are not maintained, Jewish-Israeli society will collapse upon itself and be taken over by the country's neighboring non-Jewish Palestinian Arab enemies.[36] Jacoby notes that it is through motherhood that women are able to achieve agency within the state, but that they simultaneously lose their agency because it is expected of them.[37] To support women's opportunities to serve primarily as mothers while also contributing to their household income, the country has developed labor laws which stipulated that women would be permitted to have full-time careers with limited hours so that they could pick up their children from school at the end of the school day.[38] Since it was women, and not men, who were expected to have workdays of this nature, a form of enforced femininity became inscribed into the collective consciousness of many women with regards to their roles in society. Additionally, the country's labor laws helped codify national gendered narratives that facilitated opportunities for men to establish their careers and to become prominent in establishing social and public policies while simultaneously limiting women's access to these fields by dint of their familial responsibilities.[39] Feminine identifications with motherhood were also reinforced in numerous Israeli films, with women regularly "offering up their wombs to the state" as their way of contributing to the nation-building exercise.[40]

In the decades following the establishment of the country, the Israeli army became the site where gender became most clearly delineated and also most fiercely contested. As noted above, since the country's founding, both men and women have been conscripted into the Israeli army. This statement is often used laudatorily in order to demonstrate the ways that Israeli society is equally inclusive for both men and women. While it is a mostly true statement, pertinent and relevant details are omitted that make the claim significantly less accurate and more spurious. Approximately 30 per cent of military-aged men do not serve in the military;[41] the majority of this group are ultra-Orthodox men, a group that the country has extended military exemptions to since the country's founding. In lieu of military service, these ultra-Orthodox men study in *yeshivot*, or religious seminaries. Additionally, women who are pregnant or married are also exempt from service. Also, any woman who claims she is religious (without having to prove religious observance) is also exempt. Recent figures reveal that 44 per cent of military-age women do not serve in the army.[42] More significantly, until very recently, women were barred from serving in combat units, and it was not until 1978 that women were even permitted to train male soldiers in combat courses.[43] Initial expectations of women in the army were that they were to serve as substitute mothers, nurturing and establishing a home-like atmosphere on the base for the male soldiers who were away from their mothers for extended periods of time, and performing this role has persisted for many female soldiers to this day.[44] Inequal access to elite units hindered women from being able to assume prominent roles within the army and to actually be on par with their male colleagues. This reality led to legislation in 2000 which opened all military professions to women, including serving in front-line units.[45] And yet, as Orna Sasson-Levy has suggested, even these women – who serve in the most elite units – are still subject to tokenism for being the 'woman of the unit', despite their robust qualifications which permit them to serve in the unit in the first place.[46]

As the site where hegemonic masculinity is most clearly established and performed, the Israeli military has traditionally been a site where women were not wanted, even if they were legally required to be present. In recent years, a number of legal arguments have been put forward designed to exclude women from participating in the military sphere. One of the ways that women's place in the military has been challenged is by way of questioning whether women should have the requirement to serve at all, irrespective of their personal religious or relationship status, due to an over-enlistment of soldiers.[47] Furthermore, some men – reinforcing hegemonic masculine attitudes – have challenged the 2000 law on equality by asserting that women should be ineligible to serve as pilots in the air force because they might one day become pregnant and therefore unable to serve when needed.[48] Finally, some have suggested that women's integration into the military corps presents logistical challenges for religiously observant men who might not want to serve directly alongside women, and that a woman's presence detracts from the overall atmosphere that exists between male soldiers.[49] What binds all three of these arguments together is a belief that the military is not a place where women can or should serve and that they should be excluded on the grounds of gender, irrespective of ability.

In order to combat the negative associations with female soldiers, Israeli women have embraced a number of orientations in order to better be able to integrate. Some women who serve in combat roles have typically adopted the behavior of their fellow male soldiers, practicing forms of exaggerated masculinity or hypermasculinity in order to be one of the boys.[50] These women perform gender in a way that more easily allows their male counterparts to see them for their similarities and not as a distinct and different member of the community of soldiers. Sasson-Levy understands women's adoption of masculine traits as a further entrenchment of hegemonic masculinity. While the female soldiers' regendering does permit them to integrate into the army, the choice to perform gender anew is not one of purposeful and intentional "subversion" of the military code but one of "collaboration with the military androcentric discourse"[51] because it suggests that the *only* way to effectively serve alongside men is to become like men.

The second type of role that some women have assumed in order to counter the negative associations with female soldiers involves leaning in and fully performing an exaggerated form of hegemonic femininity. By embracing their roles as surrogate mothers for the men on the base, the women become accepted and recognized as females. Orlee Hauser's fascinating research into this community of soldiers has revealed that for many, performing their military service by embracing hegemonic femininity provides meaning and substance to their service. This is because they feel that instead of being a token combat soldier who might never be fully accepted, providing comfort and familiarity to the male soldiers allows the women to feel that they are making a significant contribution to the military establishment. By choosing to embrace their femininity and to use it to positively impact the lives of their fellow soldiers, the women argue that they are actually more useful and team-oriented than the women who adopted masculine traits while serving as outliers within the military establishment.[52] The significance of the women's ideological orientation to their femininity is that they believe they are not performing femininity because it is how the state has historically defined them; instead, they are voluntarily choosing to perform femininity such that it allows them to serve their country in a way that is both personally meaningful and beneficial to the country.

Female soldiers are not the only community of women who have worked to shift perceptions of femininity away from maternal associations.[53] This has been accomplished by either embracing and framing maternal femininity in positive ways or by rejecting it outright and favoring alternative femininities. The former category includes women who work in the Israeli hi-tech sector. Despite the expectation from some that they prioritize their families over their employers, Frenkel has identified examples of women who reject this dichotomy, choosing instead to sacrifice personal time in the evenings after their children are asleep so as to further their careers. While still accepting the default orientation of women as caregivers, these women perform a redefined femininity in which they make active choices about how they prioritize their time and determine what sacrifices they make in order to do so. Working after-hours allows them to come closer to their male colleagues with regards to the quantity of work they complete, thereby allowing them to more ably compete for promotions with these male colleagues.[54] A more surprising example of the embracement of traditional femininity was discovered by Einat Lachover, Shosh Davidson, and Ornit Ramati Dvir. Following the release of the film *Wonder Woman*, the researchers studied how young Israeli girls thought about Gal Gadot, the film's Israeli star. To their surprise, they discovered not only that some of the young girls believed that Gadot performed femininity in a hegemonically Israeli way, but that they revered her for it. Locating this in Gadot's minimal use of social media, her fairly traditional style of dress, and the way she positively presented Israeliness, they saw Gadot as similar to their own mothers. Gadot's place as someone who is committed to her family and to her country reflects traditional notions of femininity, even though she is a global superstar, and the girls loved and respected her for it; appreciating her for these traits reinforces traditional hegemonic femininity but casts it in a positive light.[55]

The second way that women are challenging hegemonic femininity is by purposefully encroaching on territory that has traditionally been considered masculine, while repurposing it as either a feminine or a gender-neutral space. Esther Hertzog and Assaf Lev have identified this type of change occurring in gyms and workout classes as a by-product of the increased presence women have in these facilities and their willingness to actively resist men who refuse to allow them access to exercise spaces.[56] A third way that women have been using femininity is through the use of public protest against perceptions of government and military corruption. Most famously, the protest group Women in Black rallies in a way that subverts hegemonic femininity. By gathering in the public sphere – a traditionally masculine space – and protesting against the government and military – two traditionally masculine bodies – the women co-opt masculine domains while simultaneously reinforcing them by protesting in silence.[57] Performing femininity in this way retains elements of the hegemonic ideal – being unheard – while asserting equality by protesting in public, which was a sphere that women had hitherto not been fully invited to join as participants.

Given the limited access that women have had in Israeli society and the ways that they have often been expected to serve as supports to the men in their lives, it should not come as a complete surprise to learn that female characters have similarly been underdeveloped in much of Israeli literature. In the early years of the state and continuing into the twenty-first century, female Israeli authors received less critical and scholarly attention for their work than their male counterparts. Similarly, female characters that populate Israeli literature have tended to be significantly less dynamic than male characters. These characters have tended to be stock characters, serving to prop up male characters who feature more prominently. The absence of the feminine in the Israeli literary space can be directly linked to the ways that femininity has been constructed in Israeli society. Positioned primarily in a role that supports, nurtures, and revolves around men,[58] women – both fictional and non-fictional – were not invited to assert themselves in the public sphere of Israeli cultural and political life. For instance, Dana Olmert has identified that mothers are typically depicted only in relation to their sons who serve in the army. In this trope, the mother's duty is "caring for the soldier when he returned home on leave, taking responsibility for his food and laundry".[59] In recent years, there have been notable exceptions to this depiction. Orly Castel-Bloom's *Dolly City* envisions the mother as not a nurturer but a smothering presence; Dolly is so concerned with protecting her son that she grievously harms him. Recasting the mother in this way challenges the hegemonic ideal by suggesting that a reduction of femininity to being a stewardess whose identity is solely wrapped up in the child's life stunts growth as opposed to facilitating active and dynamic Israeli femininity.[60] A further example of a literary mother who behaves contrary to the norm is Ora in David Grossman's *To the End of the Land*. Worried that her son Ofer will be killed during his military service, Ora sets out on a cross-country journey, believing that if she is not home to greet the military chaplain bearing news of Ofer's death, then he cannot die. By not fulfilling her hegemonic duty to wait for her son's return, Ora assumes an altered feminine identity. This new identity still revolves around her relationship to her son but recasts femininity as an active role and envisions women as capable of fighting and saving their sons even as those very same sons fight on behalf of the state against its enemies.[61]

Within Israel, high rates of literacy and of interest in reading fiction led to works being published in Hebrew acquiring a "high order of cultural capital capable of motivating individuals".[62] Considered alongside a strong civic-minded population, politics and literature are interwoven and the two often impact upon each other in the shaping of Israeli national narratives.[63] In the early years of the state, cultural and literary works tended to reinforce the hegemonic narratives – including ones about gender – that were espoused. These works favored narratives and narrations that supported the national story and excluded perspectives that went contrary to the story the country wanted told about itself. Harris suggests that, following the devastating results of the Yom Kippur War in 1973, authors and film directors began to more actively question and critique the nation's foundational stories.[64] Today, works of this critical nature continue to be produced alongside works which continue to promote the traditional national narratives.

The community of Israelis who produce and publish graphic novels is very small in comparison to countries with a stronger comics tradition like the United States, Japan, France and Belgium. And while Stephen E. Tabachnick has suggested that Israel has a "highly developed graphic-novel culture",[65] there are very few original works published on a yearly basis, and even fewer that find their way to the international market in English translation. Historically, unlike other creative fields like literature, poetry, and drama, comics and cartoons were considered part of the domain of children. The emphasis on producing comics intended for children began even before the state was founded through the publication of the children's magazine *Itonenu Le'Ktanim* (Our Paper for Children). *Itonenu Le'Ktanim* featured the first original Israeli comics series, *Mickey Mouse v'Eliyahu*, and inspired the creation of *Davar Le'Yeladim* (Something for Children), Israel's most famous children's magazine. In *Davar Le'Yeladim*, writer Lea Goldberg and illustrator Arye Navon produced a comic featuring Uri Muri, one of Israel's first original characters.

In the 1950s, comics continued to be published in children's magazines, and authors and artists began to adopt elements of the American comics tradition by transposing superheroes into the Israeli milieu. These superheroes included Gidi Gezer (Gidi Carrot), a child who fought alongside Israeli soldiers against the British and Arabs in Israel's Independence War using powers he gained from eating carrots. Following the Yom Kippur War in 1973, alternative comics designed for mature readers were published. Early examples of adult-oriented texts include Uri Fink's *Profile 107*, which is a series set in an alternative and futuristic Israel where superheroes help support the aims of the Israeli government, and Yaakov Kirshen's *Dry Bones*, which satirized problems in Israeli society filtered through a biblical lens.

By the 1990s, comics were a regular feature in children's publications as a result of their increased popularity. By far the most popular series was Uri Fink's *Zbeng!*, which introduced readers to a group of students and their weekly exploits. The series was a critical success in Israel and spawned a number of spinoffs including television programs, full-length comics, novels, and other merchandise. But it was also in the 1990s that comics began to gain traction among adult readers. A confluence of factors led to this, including support from Etgar Keret – one of Israel's most popular authors – when he participated in a project that turned his short stories into comics, some of which were later published in the collected book *Jetlag*. Additionally, the formation of Actus Tragicus in 1995 established the country's first comics collective and publishing community. The group was founded by Rutu Modan and Yirmi Pinkus, and also included Itzik Rennert, Mira Friedmann, and Batia Kolton. Actus oversaw all aspects of publishing from the initial idea to the finished printed work. The group's yearly publications introduced local and international audiences to Israeli comics and helped garner praise for the very small Israeli comics community.[66] The members of Actus did not see themselves as solely comics artists; they were agents of change who "transformed how comics were perceived and produced in Israel ... [by showing comics] as substantive works of culture [and] as real books".[67] Many of the members – including Modan and Pinkus – of Actus Tragicus learned their craft at Israel's prestigious Bezalel Academy of Arts and Design, where they were taught by Belgian writer-illustrator Michel Kichka. Kichka's style was heavily influenced by the European comics tradition, and he introduced this style to the new generation of Israeli cartoonists who envisioned a more serious and mature Israeli comics culture.

The community of graphic novel writers and illustrators remained primarily relegated to the margins of Israeli culture for much of the country's first 55 years. While this led to only limited recognition, it allowed for experimenting and exploring with minimal intervention and oversight. The creators were able to establish their own distinct comics style and personality without external expectations. Beginning in the first decade of the twenty-first century, two Israeli comic artists and graphic novelists garnered significant international attention for their work. Both Rutu Modan and Asaf Hanuka have won Eisner Awards. Modan has twice won Best Original Graphic Novel, first for *Exit Wounds* and then for *The Property*, while Hanuka won the award for Best American Edition of an International Text for his editorial cartoon series "The Realist".

Despite the increased international attention, comics and graphic novels still do not receive the same type of fanfare or attention within Israeli society as other forms of media. As a nation, Israelis are known to be vociferous readers, but comics and graphic novels have not yet made inroads into the literary market in the ways that they have in other countries. Smadar Shiffman has identified that within Israel, "poets, fiction writers, and playwrights are ... speakers for morality, conscience, and humane responsibility. They both represent the nation ... and are at a distance from it".[68] Noticeably absent in Shiffman's assessment of the writer's role in Israeli society is the graphic novelist and cartoonist. Yet in spite of minimal recognition, Israeli cartoonists and graphic novelists do also serve as agents sounding the clarion call against corruption in Israeli society. Ariel Kahn sees in the Israeli cartoonist and graphic novelist a figure who is able to consider "cultural and historical tropes from a productively marginal position".[69] As outsiders to the mainstream Israeli literary tradition and producers of a media that operates in the fringes of Israeli society, they are better positioned to call attention to problems that others might not see or might not be willing to address, and to produce works which challenge the perpetuation of these issues.

Despite a publication history of almost 50 years, creative works that challenge the hegemonic narratives have not had tremendous impact in changing Israeli society. This is because the early Israeli narratives "became signifiers for the Israeli reality and created a language representing the hegemony of the Zionist narrative. Despite ideological changes, these earlier images of Zionism continue to possess meaning".[70] And yet these counter-narratives continue to be published. According to Harris, a dominant theme of the Israeli fiction that challenges hegemonies is an exploration of "the imagined origins of its nation, ultimately reflecting on the failure of its ideals".[71] Despite a national ethos that prides sacrifice, heroism, and contribution to the nation, a growing body of texts depict Israelis committing suicide as a way to challenge these hegemonies.[72] Similarly, the imperative of participating willingly in the army has led to the creation of films which challenge conscription. Works like these, suggests Yosef, reinforce the harsh and brutal realities of war and the ways that war negatively impacts the lives of soldiers and citizenry despite the nation's continued insistence on lionizing its soldiers.[73] I contend that comics and graphic novels produced by Israelis about Israel serve as disruptive counter-narratives which challenge hegemonic discourses. The central thesis of this book is that a prominent feature of Israeli comics and graphic novels is a deconstruction of hegemonic gender constructs and an establishment of alternative gendered identities for men and women. Through the visualization of a different Israel, comics and graphic novels by Israelis depict an Israel that is similar to the one that currently exists but is different in a significant way. These texts shift the dominant portrayal of gender away from hypermasculinity and docile femininity and towards a new gendered construct. Illustrations serve as a powerful tool, facilitating the envisioning of this new society, leading the reader not only to think about a new society, but to actually see this society.

Israeli graphic novels have been studied by a number of comics scholars in the last few years. This is the first book-length study of the Israeli graphic novel genre as a whole. In my selection of texts to consider, I cast a wide net, relying on three key criteria: first, the texts needed to be produced by Israelis. Second, the texts needed to focus on Israeli society. Combined, these two criteria position this book as one about what Israelis have to say about their own society. Therefore, texts written about Israel by non-Israelis are not included, and nor are graphic novels by Israelis but not about Israel or Israeli identity.[74] Third, as a book about Israelis but intended for an international audience, I have primarily limited myself to texts that have been published in both Hebrew *and* English and that are still in print.[75] With the exception of texts that are analyzed in the third chapter, all of the comics and graphic novels mentioned in this book are available in at least Hebrew and English, but many of them have been subsequently translated into even more languages.

It is important to note at the outset the diversity of authors and illustrators whose work is considered in this book. The authors and illustrators include both men and women, secular and religious, and of different sexual orientations. As well, the texts were first published in different languages, with some in Hebrew, and others in English or French. There is a variety of genres, including semi-autobiography, fiction, full-length graphic novels, weekly editorial, adaptation from short story, and adaptation from a feature film. The diversity of author, genre, and language of publication reflect a range of perspectives that can be brought to bear on Israeli society. And while the authors and artists do not produce a uniform message about gender in Israel, what links them together is a rejection of the dominant narrative that has been established and told about masculinity and femininity in Israeli society.

I would be remiss to not mention two communities who do not feature in this book. Both Palestinian-Israeli and ultra-Orthodox *haredi* texts are not considered. The decision to not include texts by either community was made by necessity. Neither community has produced graphic novels that indicate an engagement with Israeli society, and, as communities that often sit at the fringes of Israeli society, they rarely factor into or feature in any graphic novels produced by Israelis from other communities. Graphic novels produced by members of the ultra-Orthodox community focus on either depictions of daily religious life or of biblical and rabbinic texts.[76] This genre of texts strips away the Israeli locale and establishes religious identity as the primary signifier in the texts, and therefore these graphic novels fall outside the scope of this project. With regards to gender norms, here, too, it is difficult to make many observations about these two communities since they are understudied populations who differ greatly from other Jewish-Israeli communities. As a society rooted in Arab traditions, Palestinian-Israeli gender norms differ from Jewish-Israeli gender norms.[77] With regards to ultra-Orthodox Israelis, the community serves as a unique gendered foil to established gender hegemonies in Israeli society. Whereas the Israeli male eschewed the study hall in favor of developing the land and fighting on the battlefield, ultra-Orthodox Israelis remain committed to many of the gendered stereotypes that Israelis rejected in the state's formative years. Recent studies about ultra-Orthodox Jewish Israelis have explored how gender has been performed in specific sites, for example, relating to women in the workforce[78] or sexual desires,[79] but comprehensive theories of the performance of gender in contemporary *haredi* society have not yet been published.

In the first chapter of the book, I turn to *Waltz with Bashir*, *Exit Wounds*, "The Realist", and *Pizzeria Kamikaze* to identify alternative ways of envisioning masculinity within Israeli society. In Chapter 2, I turn my attention to femininity and how it is depicted in graphic novels. I examine "The Realist", *The Property*, and *Farm 54* in order to establish the different models of femininity that graphic novelists have produced. Lastly, in the third chapter, I identify the ways that Hebrew-language Israeli graphic novels offer further examples of progressive gender and identity politics. This is accomplished by analyzing Michel Kichka's *Second Generation: Things I Didn't Tell My Father* and *Falafel with Hot Sauce*, Ilana Zeffren's short stories "Holidays" and "Zina", and Shay Charka's *Beyond the Line*.

By exploring the texts in light of classical gender constructs, I move beyond facilely comparing and contrasting texts with Jewish-Israeli gender norms. The Israeli literary scene is replete with examples that have worked alongside the hegemony by depicting it and therefore reinforcing it by normalizing it. Instead, Israeli graphic novels are transgressive in the ways that they actively challenge the hegemony and depict alternative constructions of gender. I contend that Israeli fictional and semi-fictional graphic novels envision and portray alternative gendered realities through the use of visual signifiers which serve as social disrupters, mapping out new gendered spaces for Israelis and facilitating spaces where people like Carmi and the anonymous social worker are not judged in relation to societal expectations about how men and women are supposed to behave. Given the army's central position within Israeli society and its place as a prime mechanism for establishing gender norms, it should not come as a surprise that many of these alternative genderings occur in relation to the role of the soldier.

This work operates in conversation with the wider field of comics and graphic novel studies and the ways that gender has been explored. As a visual medium, comics and graphic novels provide an opportunity not only to read the performance of gender but to see it as well. As this book focuses on depictions of either real-life people or people who could be real, my exploration of gender will not involve an interrogation of superhero comics and what Ross Murray has termed the "proliferating parody of gender 'norms'" in superhero comics where the characters "perform and display hypermasculine and hyperfeminine roles and forms".[80] Instead, my study more naturally operates in conversation with scholars who consider gendered positions in graphic novels that are designed to reflect – in some way – the real world. This includes analyses of distinctly Jewish and Israeli works as well as texts that explore other ethnic, national, and racial communities. Much like this book and its focus on gender in Israel and how Israeli graphic novelists challenge hegemonic notions of gender, Stella Oh's work has demonstrated how Gene Luen Yang's *American Born Chinese* deconstructs gender identities among Chinese American men through an appropriation of stereotypes foisted upon them by fellow Americans.[81] Among scholars of Jewish graphic novels, Tahneer Oksman's excellent analysis of American Jewish women's autobiographical comics, *"How Come Boys Get to Keep Their Noses?"*, serves as an important foil for my own exploration of gender in Israeli graphic novels. Oksman suggests that female graphic novelists – much like Israeli graphic novelists – operate within a marginalized community and that this facilitates opportunities for greater creative expression and license that allow them to "respond to and reinvent the ways that Jewish American identity has been constructed".[82]

Before beginning the book, a note about myself as author: I am not an Israeli citizen, yet I am writing about Israel and Israelis. In addition to publishing numerous academic articles about Israeli graphic novels, I have spent the majority of my professional life teaching about Israeli society to North Americans and have authored a number of studies about Israeli education. I have spent considerable time living in Israel and among Israelis and am proficient in Hebrew and therefore have tried – wherever possible – to read the texts included in this study in their original language. As well, I am aware of my own identity as a cis-gender heterosexual male writing about femininity and LGBTQ+ communities. Wherever possible, I have tried to write in a sensitive and respectful manner given the hurt and pain that many have experienced – both inside Israel and in the wider world – because of gender-based violence and discrimination. It is my fervent desire that the progressive and inclusive visions presented by Israeli graphic novelists will one day lead to the end of hatred and persecution in all of its pernicious permutations.

Notes

1 *Economist,* "Mission Unaccomplished".
2 *Times of Israel*, "Israel's Virus-Battered Economy".
3 Knell, "Netanyahu Focus".
4 Peled, "What Became".
5 *Times of Israel*, "Topless Protester".
6 Peled, "What Became".
7 Peled, "What Became".
8 Brown, "Topless Protest".
9 Ploskov, "Not like this".
10 Harris, *An Ideological Death.*
11 Harris, *An Ideological Death*, 5.
12 Boyarin, *Unheroic Conduct*, 2.
13 Cited in Kroha, *The Drama*, 32.
14 Kroha, *The Drama*, 23.
15 Gilman, "The Jewish Body", 589.
16 Hirsch, "Hummus Masculinity in Israel", 351.
17 Boyarin, *Unheroic Conduct*, 4.
18 Biale, *Eros and the Jews*, 176.
19 Spector-Mersel, "Never-aging Stories", 73.
20 Kaplan, "The Military", 127.
21 Lomsky-Feder and Rapoport, "Juggling Models of Masculinity", 115.
22 Carmit Yefet, "Feminism and Hyper-Masculinity", 57-58.

23 Schwartz, "The Person, the Path", 324.
24 Carmit Yefet, "Feminism and Hyper-Masculinity", 53.
25 Carmit Yefet, "Feminism and Hyper-Masculinity", 58.
26 Yosef, "Spectacles of Pain", 51.
27 Sion and Ben-Ari, "Imagined Masculinity", 22.
28 Lomsky-Feder and Rapoport, "Juggling Models of Masculinity", 115.
29 Spector-Mersel, "Never-aging Stories", 72.
30 Sharim, "Choreographing Masculinity", 136.
31 Biale, *Eros and the Jews*, 187.
32 Lachover, Davidson and Ramati Dvir, "The Authentic Conservative", 4.
33 Blumen and Halevi, "Staging Peace", 978.
34 Hirsch and Grosswirth Kachtan, "Is 'Hegemonic Masculinity'", 692.
35 Jacoby, *Women in Zones*, 7.
36 Frenkel, "Reprogramming Femininity", 355.
37 Jacoby, *Women in Zones*, 8.
38 Frenkel, "Reprogramming Femininity", 355.
39 Jacoby, *Women in Zones*, 37.
40 Harris, *Warriors, Witches, Whores*, 70.
41 Ahronheim, "A Third".
42 Ahronheim, "A Third".
43 Jacoby, "Fighting in the Feminine", 83.
44 Hauser, "We Rule the Base", 626–627.
45 Jacoby, "Fighting in the Feminine", 83.
46 Sasson-Levy, "Constructing Identities", 370.
47 Jacoby, "Fighting in the Feminine", 86.
48 Jacoby, "Fighting in the Feminine", 86.
49 Jacoby, "Fighting in the Feminine", 86.
50 Sasson-Levy, "Constructing Identities", 357–358.
51 Sasson-Levy, "Constructing Identities", 371.
52 Hauser, "We Rule the Base", 645.
53 Hertzog and Lev, "Male Dominance under Threat".
54 Frenkel, "Reprogramming Femininity", 365–368.
55 Lachover, Davidson and Ramati Dvir, "The Authentic Conservative", 13.
56 Hertzog and Lev, "Male Dominance under Threat".
57 Blumen and Halevi, "Staging Peace", 979.
58 Fuchs, "Gender, War".
59 Olmert, "Mothers of Soldiers", 342.
60 Olmert, "Mothers of Soldiers", 352–354.
61 Rachel S. Harris has noted a similar sentiment about female characters in Israeli cinema who serve as props to male characters. She writes: "trapped within their own social milieu, these women are powerless to effect change". And yet, like Dolly and Ora, recent military films do show an expansion of notions of femininity and a rejection of the traditional hegemonic model. See Harris, "Parallel Lives", 80.
62 Harris, *An Ideological Death*, 8.
63 Harris, *An Ideological Death*, 19.

64 Harris, *An Ideological Death*, 8–9.
65 Tabachnick, "The Jewish Graphic Novel", 449.
66 Much of the material contained in this overview comes from chapters one and two from Haworth, *The Comics of Rutu Modan*, and from Eshed's website "Hebrew Comics – A History", which includes a history of comics in Israel.
67 Haworth, *The Comics of Rutu Modan*, 51 and 53.
68 Shiffman, "'If not Now, When?'", 70.
69 Kahn, "From Darkness into Light", 198.
70 Harris, *An Ideological Death,* 16.
71 Harris, *An Ideological Death*, 10.
72 Harris, *An Ideological Death*, 10.
73 Yosef, "Spectacles of Pain", 53.
74 Examples of graphic novels by non-Israelis about Israel include Sarah Glidden's *How to Understand Israel in 60 Days or Less*, Harvey Pekar and J.T. Waldman's *Not the Israel My Parents Promised Me*, Boaz Yakin and Nick Bertozzi's *Jerusalem: A Family Portrait*, Joe Sacco's *Palestine* and *Footnotes in Gaza*, and Guy Delisle's *Jerusalem*. Examples of graphic novels by Israelis but not about Israel include Koren Shadmi's *The Abaddon*, Asaf Hanuka, Tomer Hanuka and Boaz Lavie's *The Divine*, Ari Folman and David Polonsky's *Anne Frank's Diary: The Graphic Adaptation* and Yehuda and Maya Devir's *One of These Days*.
75 Examples of graphic novels produced by Israelis about Israel which have not been translated into English include Ilana Zeffren's *Pink Story* and *Rishumon*, Eli Eshed and Uri Fink's *HaGolem*, and Shay Charka's *Beyond the Line*. Many of the original Actus Comics collections are, unfortunately, no longer in print and can only be accessed on the second-hand market. This includes the wonderful collection *How to Love*, which contains a number of stories that interrogate notions of gender in Israeli society. Due to its unavailability, I have chosen to not include it in my analysis, but interested readers should definitely check the book out, especially Batia Kolton's "Summer Story", Mira Friedmann's "Independence Day", and Rutu Modan's "Your Number One Fan".
76 Barron, "The Comic Books".
77 Popper-Giveon, Keshet, and Liberman, "Increasing Gender".
78 Raz and Tzruya, "Doing Gender".
79 Stadler and Taragin-Zeller, "Like a Snake".
80 Murray, "The Feminine Mystique", 59.
81 Oh, "Laughter Against Laughter".
82 Oksman, *How Come Boys,* 10.

1 Complex masculinities and the not-so-macho man in Israeli graphic novels

Matt Reingold

Situated within a society that established its gender norms primarily with regards to how men should behave, Israeli graphic novels have offered a number of alternative constructions of masculine identity. In this chapter, I explore four graphic novels set during different periods of Israel's history. What links them together is a consistent refrain that the hegemonic model that carried the country from its infancy through its first 65 years is no longer applicable or effective for understanding the myriad ways that men perform their body politics. Instead, texts that challenge the primacy of the narrative of the soldier who bravely sacrifices himself for the nation and of the strong and emotionally distant man are dismissed as irrelevant for today's Israeli male. In their place are masculine constructs which recognize the importance of vulnerability, fatherhood, insecurity, and compassion. These texts depict men who grapple with what it means to be a man in the twenty-first century, and while they do not arrive at the same conclusions or identities, their results demonstrate the constructions of multiple sites of masculinity within Israeli society.

The four texts that I will be focusing on in this chapter are Ari Folman and David Polonsky's *Waltz with Bashir*, Rutu Modan's *Exit Wounds*, Etgar Keret and Asaf Hanuka's *Pizzeria Kamikaze*, and Asaf Hanuka's "The Realist".[1] *Waltz with Bashir* is an autobiographical exploration of Ari Folman's inability to remember his role as a soldier during Israel's war with Lebanon in 1982 and his quest to recover his memories and discover whether he participated in a massacre against Palestinian civilians. Set against the backdrop of the Second Palestinian Intifada which occurred from 2000 to 2005, *Exit Wounds* is a story about Numi, a young Israeli woman who encourages her fellow Israeli Koby to try to determine whether his estranged father Gabriel was killed in a recent suicide bombing. *Pizzeria Kamikaze* is a story set in a fictional Tel Aviv necropolis where all of the city's residents are individuals who

DOI: 10.4324/9781003150435-2

died by suicide. There, Mordy first tries to find his former girlfriend Desiree, but eventually realizes that he is actually in love with Leehee, a woman that he has met in the afterlife following his suicide. Lastly, Asaf Hanuka's "The Realist" is an editorial cartoon series that is published in the Israeli economic newspaper *Calcalist*. Each weekly installment addresses how Hanuka navigates an issue or challenge that is affecting his life. Sometimes these are national issues, like the schism between secular and religious Jews or the high cost of living, but oftentimes they are personal issues, like how to raise his children or how to communicate effectively with his wife.

Compassionate soldiers in Ari Folman and David Polonsky's *Waltz with Bashir*

Waltz with Bashir (2009) revolves around former Israel Defence Forces (IDF) soldier Ari Folman's discovery that he possesses no memories from his time spent serving in Lebanon during the 1982 First Lebanon War. Among the texts considered in this chapter, it is the one that most directly questions the masculine nature of Israeli soldiers and the ways that young men are expected to perform heroic masculinity on the battlefield. Over the course of the work, Folman deconstructs many of the central tenets of Israeli masculinity, especially the ways that soldiers are lionized for their bravery and commitment to the country. Folman worries that he must have done something so terrible and awful that his mind has blocked out the memory in order to protect himself from his own violent crimes. In order to determine the truth, Folman meets with fellow soldiers with whom he served in Lebanon, a psychologist who specializes in recovering lost memories, and a television reporter who was on the scene in Lebanon during the war. The text rapidly cuts across time and space, creating a feeling of disambiguation that mirrors Folman's own uncertainties. Eventually, Folman comes to learn that while he did not directly play a role in the deaths of Palestinians in the refugee camps of Sabra and Shatila he knew what was happening during the attacks. To his horror and shame, he remembers that he saw the crimes being committed because he lit flares so that the Christian Lebanese militia could see at night while they were murdering Palestinians.

Waltz with Bashir was originally released as an animated Hebrew-language film in 2008 and published as an English-language graphic novel shortly thereafter in 2009 by Metropolitan Books. Both the film and graphic novel were produced by the Israeli team of director Ari Folman and illustrator David Polonsky. The two have subsequently collaborated on an animated film about Anne Frank and a graphic novel adaptation of her famous diary. *Waltz with Bashir* has received considerable scholarly and popular attention. The film won the 2009 Golden Globe Award for Best Foreign Language Film and its Israeli equivalent, the Ophir, in 2008. It was also nominated for dozens of additional awards at film festivals and ceremonies including the 2008 Cannes Film Festival, the 2009 Academy Awards, and the 2009 BAFTAs. Given *Waltz with Bashir*'s initial release in Hebrew, the text is primarily designed by Israelis and for Israelis. In the work, Folman draws a portrait of the Israeli soldier at his most vulnerable. While deeply personal, the text is also an indictment of the nation and its leadership for the way that it conducted itself during the First Lebanon War. Visually, the graphic novel is a collection of the stills from the animated film. Bodily depictions are raw and edgy, with dark and rough shading throughout. Folman and Polonsky employ a number of aesthetic features throughout the text. These include splash pages which highlight and emphasize certain actions and small, highly condensed panels which slow the pacing down, forcing the reader to carefully parse the events that took place in Lebanon.

In his depictions of soldiers and their experiences, Folman challenges hegemonic Israeli attitudes towards both the military and masculinity. In Folman, Yael Munk sees an author whose work is "unprecedented" in Israeli society for his willingness to "come to terms with a terrible, repressed traumatic past … and the atrocities carried out in the name of his country, the country that he as a soldier represented".[2] Rachel S. Harris locates *Waltz with Bashir* as part of an extended Israeli creative process by filmmakers who challenge the nation's foundational myths.[3] As noted in the introduction, given that the military is the main way that socialization occurs for men in Israeli society, it therefore also creates the dominant construct of masculinity for the country. This masculinity is one that is aggressive and confident, and that is built on the backs of young men who are willing to sacrifice their lives for the greater good of the nation. Philip Hollander identifies in the way that Folman speaks to his friends, listens to their words, and builds a community around empathy and nurturing a direct challenge to the ways that masculinity has been historically constructed in the state.[4]

A central feature of *Waltz with Bashir*'s critique of traditional Israeli masculinity is the way that the relationship between the soldiers is depicted as one where they care, and where they consider the psychological impact of their actions on each other. Hollander has noted how *Waltz with Bashir* "expands the masculine purview by stressing the importance of biological paternity and male nurturing".[5] Early in the text, Boaz Rein, one of Folman's fellow soldiers, explains to him that during their encampment he was dispatched to kill a group of dogs that might alert the Lebanese to the Israeli soldiers' presence. Boaz explains that he was chosen for this role because "[his commander] knew [he] was incapable of shooting people".[6] Despite being illustrated with eyes wide with fear, Boaz's vulnerability and inability to fulfil a central component of soldierly duty, that is, shooting an enemy to kill him, does not earn him derision or scorn. Instead, his fellow soldiers find other, more palatable roles for him within the confines of the army. While the nature of brotherhood within the army is to be expected, that even someone who so clearly fails to live up to the hegemonic ideal is welcomed suggests an alternative understanding of what the bond that actually exists is.

What emerges most clearly from *all* of the soldiers' wartime recollections is that Boaz is not an outlier. While other soldiers might have been more willing to pull the trigger than Boaz, each soldier fails – in some very real way – to live up to the hegemonic ideal. For example, Carmi worries that "everyone around [him] was screwing like rabbits while [he] was the nerd winning all the chess competitions".[7] Folman is angry his girlfriend has dumped him while he is a soldier away at war and he hopes he dies so that she feels guilty forever. The soldier sitting next to Ronnie Dayag was shot and Ronnie failed to return fire and instead ran away. In his moment of panic, he worries about his mom and what she will do without him. Ronnie eventually finds his way back to his platoon after wandering for miles around Lebanon's beaches, and even though he "had the feeling they saw [him] as someone who'd deserted his friends",[8] this is not how his fellow soldiers treat him, as they welcome him back and celebrate that he is still alive. Even though Carmi notes that he thought he was "the only one with masculinity problems",[9] the platoon's behaviors suggest that everyone struggles with the impossible expectations foisted upon them by Israeli society, and that they all know this on some level even if they fail to verbalize it and actively discuss it. Protecting Boaz and not shunning him, and welcoming Ronnie back and not humiliating him, reinforce the notion of militaristic brotherhood, but these incidents challenge the nature of that brotherhood as one not built on shared manly experiences but as one that recognizes the isolation that each feels and the need to protect each other from those outside of the troop who might question their masculine identities.

The ultimate failure to critically engage with their fears and worries is what leads to the lingering psychological wounds from their time in the army. Because of the weight of masculine expectations, no one spoke to Ronnie about how he was feeling about knowing he did not defend his fellow soldiers the way he was expected to, and as a result, he still feels guilty when he visits military cemeteries, and he ultimately still feels alone. In one of the most haunting images of the text, Ronnie is depicted as himself in the present, walking the deserted Lebanese coast of 1985, looking for his fellow soldiers (Figure 1.1). Despite the passage of time, Ronnie remains stuck in 1985. Similarly, everyone's inability to remember where they were during the war's most infamous moments outside the Sabra and Shatila refugee camps reinforces the psychological wounds that the young men experienced. This inability to remember that they were perched atop rooftops lighting the night's sky testifies to their unpreparedness for war and for serving as soldiers in a war that they neither understood nor wanted to be a part of. The platoon, suggests Folman, is not a group of macho men who have set out to defend the country. Instead, they are a group of young men who have been assigned a task that challenges their morals and ethics and for which they are unprepared.

At one point, Folman and his fellow soldiers try to call attention to the massacre of Palestinians but are rebuffed by the Israeli political elite. Gorging on steak served on fine china, Israeli Minister of Defence Ariel Sharon is depicted as indifferent to both the physical devastation of Palestinian lives and also the psychological devastation of his troops who want to stop the massacre but are told to stay clear of it. Writing about this scene, Hollander persuasively argues that men like Sharon perform "amoral masculinity" through the "maintenance of outdated masculine standards".[10] Remaining committed to the hegemonic ideal

Figure 1.1 Ronnie walking on the Lebanese beach. Credit: Ari Folman and David Polonsky, *Waltz with Bashir* (New York: Metropolitan Books, 2009): 45.

of soldierly masculinity among Israeli soldiers obfuscates the reality of the soldiers' experiences and ultimately comes to harm the soldiers, both affecting them when they are serving in combat and causing their inability to successfully navigate their post-army lives, given how deeply so many of the men featured in *Waltz with Bashir* remain psychologically wounded in the present. It is only through Folman's willingness to talk to his fellow soldiers, to provide them opportunities to unburden themselves from their traumas and histories, that they are all able to collectively remember what happened and to begin the process of healing from the First Lebanon War.

Reconciling Romantics in Rutu Modan's *Exit Wounds*

Published by Drawn & Quarterly in 2007 and a recipient of the prestigious Eisner Award, Rutu Modan's *Exit Wounds* is a story set during the Second Palestinian Intifada which took place in Israel between September 2000 and February 2005. Modan is a graduate of the Bezalel Academy of Art and Design, and she serves as a professor in its communication department. Modan's significance within the Israeli comics scene cannot be understated. In addition to publishing the Eisner-winning *Exit Wounds* and *The Property* (which is explored in the following chapter) and teaching comic book writing, Modan is a founding member of Actus Tragicus. Modan has also established Noah Books, a publishing house that reissues classic Israeli children's books with new artwork. The imprint is designed to introduce young Israelis to some of the most famous early-state characters like Uri Cadduri and to create graphic novel-type books for younger audiences.

Set against the backdrop of suicide bombings during the Second Palestinian Intifada, *Exit Wounds* revolves around a burgeoning romance between Koby, a taxi driver, and Numi, a soldier nearing the completion of her mandatory military service. The two meet because Numi had previously dated Koby's estranged father Gabriel and, after not hearing from him for a period of time, becomes convinced that he was killed in a suicide bombing. As Koby and Numi search for Gabriel, the two develop feelings for each other and discover that Gabriel was not killed, and that he had in fact left Numi for another woman. Modan employs a rich palette of muted colors in her text that has been printed on high quality matte paper. Modan's panels tend to be illustrated in squares or rectangles, with 4–6 panels per page. On many pages, she includes panels that are horizontal and panels that are vertical, allowing the reader to see tall buildings or to see a wide-angle zoom on a scene.

Exit Wounds represents a significant progression in Modan's work with regards to how men are portrayed. In her earlier short story collection *Jamilti and other Stories*, a number of Israeli men are depicted in ways that reflect negative aspects of hegemonic masculinity. For instance, in "Jamilti", Guri, the male protagonist, is consistently dismissive of his fiancée Rama's emotional needs. He refuses to even pretend to feign interest in her wedding dress and he chooses to play soccer with his friends instead of helping with wedding arrangements like he promised. Later in the text, Guri also participates in a misogynistic conversation with a cab driver in Rama's presence where the two discuss Rama's sexual proclivities as a left-wing and pro-peace Israeli.[11] In the short story "Homecoming", Mali, the female protagonist, has her sexuality held hostage by her father-in-law Yosef, who refuses to accept that his son Gadi – and Mali's husband – has died in Lebanon and will not allow her to date anyone else. While Yosef's commitment to his son's memory as a brave Israeli soldier reflects elements of the hegemony, this commitment stifles Mali's freedom and ability to actualize her own desires. The lone character who recognizes this is Max, Mali's secret boyfriend, and his solution to Mali's problem is to pretend that an airplane that has crash-landed in their village was piloted by Gadi, but his idea falls on deaf ears and the story ends with no resolution for Mali.[12]

In *Exit Wounds*, Koby's father Gabriel also manipulates women. Gabriel is a serial-dater of marginalized women. These women – including Numi and an ultra-Orthodox woman – are either members of communities where sex is not discussed or are not traditionally beautiful and therefore suffer from insecurities. By entering sexual relationships with them simultaneously, Gabriel takes advantage of their vulnerabilities and believes that their insecurities will preclude them from questioning the attention he gives them. Where *Exit Wounds* differs from *Jamilti and Other Stories* is in how it provides not only a clear critique of the Gabriels, Guris and Yosefs of Israeli society but also a response to their behavior in the form of Koby.

Throughout *Exit Wounds*, Modan constantly disrupts notions of hegemonic gender norms that are prevalent in Israeli society. On the first page of the text, the reader is introduced to Koby mid-yawn as he sits in his cab waiting for a customer. The profession, while necessary within a society, is one of passivity. As a cabdriver, Koby sits in his cab all day waiting for passengers to require his services. In this role, he is dependent on their decisions to dictate his destination. In a scene later in the text, Koby's cab breaks down while he is driving Numi, and in this moment of opportunity to demonstrate his manliness by fixing the car and impressing Numi with his abilities, Koby is unable to repair it. He is forced to be dependent on another man to solve his problem in front of his prospective partner. Conversely, it is Numi who more clearly embodies an occupation that is reflective of hegemonic masculinity. Unlike the traditional dichotomy in which men serve in the army and women wait patiently for their return,[13] as an Israeli soldier, Numi is serving her country during a period of violence and terrorism. Even though Numi is serving in the army stationed at a desk position and not on the front lines, she is working to defend Israeli citizens from harm while Koby shuttles people around the city in a taxicab. Koby's occupation is antithetical both to the role of the soldier and to how masculinity is constructed in Israel. Moshe Levy, Einat Hollander and Smadar Noy-Canyon have suggested that masculinity is identified with "self-control, courage, independence, achievement-oriented risk taking and a striving for victory"[14] and that the inverse traits are reflective of femininity. In Koby's inability to solve his own problems and even with regards to his vocational choices, Modan's character evidences far more feminine traits than Numi, who possesses the very traits that Koby lacks.

The gender reversals extend far beyond the two central characters' occupations. While Koby has a favorite sports team that he likes to watch, and enjoying team sports is considered a component of Israeli masculinity,[15] Numi's family actually owns the team. Whereas Koby still lives with his aunt and uncle in a small apartment because he cannot afford to live independently, Numi lives with her parents in a lavish mansion that is guarded by two sentry dogs. Considered in isolation, the disjunction between their financial circumstances suggests merely contrasting socio-economic differences. However, considered through the lens of Israeli gender norms, Koby is presented in a non-traditional way. While romance stories of poor boys winning the hearts of wealthy girls might be an attractive narrative, it does not reflect the ways that gender has been constructed within Israeli society due to the relative positions of power and weakness that each character has. As a hero, Koby's poverty is a limiting factor that serves to emasculate, rather than empower, especially in comparison to the vast wealth that Numi's family has.

Perhaps the most significant way that Modan challenges gender norms is through her depictions of both Koby and Numi. Neither character fits the traditional model of Israeli men and women. Koby is short, pudgy and non-muscular, and he prefers baggy clothing to clothing that highlights his musculature. His is not the physique of the reserve soldier who prioritizes maintaining a healthy regimen for the benefit of the state. Similarly, unlike her mother and sister, who spend hours primping and preening in order to attract men through displays of exaggerated femininity – and who encourage her to do likewise – Numi eschews makeup, preferring to allow people to see the moles that dot her face. Furthermore, she keeps her hair cut unstylishly short and she tends to wear drab and dull clothing so as to not stand out. Nicknamed "The Giraffe" by her fellow soldiers, who are repulsed by her, Numi also stands taller than Koby (Figure 1.2). Taken together, the couple make for one of the *least* hegemonically traditional couples in Israeli litera-ture. As described by Kevin Haworth, "these are not the great pioneers of the Zionist posters of the 1930s, which featured physically striking men and women standing tall in the fields or holding rifles".[16]

In fact, Koby is initially so put off by Numi's appearance that he is disappointed when the hotel they stay at when trying to find Gabriel puts them in the same room as opposed to the two rooms that he requested. Running counter to gendered expectations in which Koby would jump at the opportunity to share a room with a woman, Haworth notes how the ironic twist further subverts Israeli norms of what to expect of men.[17] When Koby and Numi do eventually have sex, Koby's

Figure 1.2 Numi is taller than Koby. Credit: Rutu Modan, *Exit Wounds* (Montreal: Drawn & Quarterly, 2007): 13.

sexual inexperience in comparison to Numi – and in turn his diminished manliness – is evident when he is unable to even pull her underwear down. This decreases the sexual tension because Numi needs to sit up and take off her own underwear. Furthermore, in the middle of sex, Numi makes a joke about how both Koby and his father like to suck on her nipples. It is significant that it is Numi, the woman, who is making sexual jokes, and not Koby, the man, whose gendered community within Israel reveres and hallows sexual jokes as a component of hegemonic male bonding.[18] Whether Numi imbued this type of banter from her fellow soldiers in the army or from elsewhere is unknown, but what is clear from the text is that Koby appreciates neither the lewdness of the joke nor the comparison to his father's own sexual proclivities. In this situation, because the joke was personalized, the joke resulted in Koby distancing himself from Numi as opposed to bringing the two together in the ways that sexual jokes have done for Israeli soldiers on duty.[19] Koby's rejection of the joke further testifies to his discomfort with traditional aspects of hegemonic Israeli masculinity.

Like his appearance and occupation, Koby's personality and mannerisms also reflect a masculinity that is at odds with the ways that masculinity is constructed in Israeli society. This is a masculinity that is both passive and deferential. In a telling photograph from his childhood, Koby is seen hiding behind other members of his family, relegating himself to the background (Figure 1.3). As well, while Koby and Numi come from different economic backgrounds, his insistence that Numi pay for a parking ticket that was accrued during their travels is reflective of a rejection of how men are expected to behave chivalrously and to assume responsibility over financial matters. Koby is also unable to participate in meaningful conversations, such as when Numi tries to push him to articulate a position on the relationship between politics and religion in Israeli society – a topic she cares deeply about – but Koby has no opinion on the matter. He even hides his birthday from Numi, despite having spent the whole of it together. Perhaps most significantly, even when Koby is confronted with the potential reality that his estranged father has been killed in a suicide bombing, he remains reticent about calling him, preferring that others inquire on his behalf. As Koby acknowledges in a conversation with Numi, he is detached from those around him.[20] Being detached from the world and the people surrounding him and choosing instead to seek solace in solitude also runs counter to the expected norms of masculinity, because it is the man who is expected to reach out into the world and to engage with it, but this is not the way that Koby acts or behaves.

Figure 1.3 Koby hiding in the family photograph. Credit: Rutu Modan, *Exit Wounds* (Montreal: Drawn & Quarterly, 2007): 64.

While Koby initially professes that he is happy with the detached way that he lives his life, the denouement of the graphic novel suggests that Koby comes to recognize that he is not as happy as he has claimed to be. No longer dependent on Numi to lead the search for Gabriel following his decision to break up with her after her sexual joke, Koby takes the initiative on his own to find out where his father is. A further example of Koby making active choices occurs at the end of *Exit Wounds*. There, Koby returns to Numi's home and, after being chased up a tree by her dogs, explains to her that he wants them to start over and begin dating like a real couple. Despite Numi's reticence based on her own fears, she encourages Koby to take the leap – both literal and metaphorical – into her arms, promising to catch him as he jumps out from the tree. Koby's willingness to do so suggests newfound confidence and a desire to take the initiative in his relationship with Numi and is reflective of a change in the way that he performs his masculinity. Koby, as suggested by Stephen E. Tabachnick, has "learned to trust Numi ... [and has] gained confidence through their relationship".[21] More in line with traditional hegemonic depictions, Koby is now the one chasing after Numi and pushing for a relationship. He has degrees of confidence that were not evident throughout much of the text. And yet it cannot be said that Koby has come to fully embrace the hegemonic masculinity of his father or other male characters in Modan's earlier works. Koby is still a deeply wounded character who is insecure and vulnerable. What shifts within Koby following meeting Numi is a recognition that his vulnerability has become like a shield, protecting him from being hurt but also sequestering him from those he might form relationships with. As Koby lowers his defenses and allows himself to be vulnerable with Numi, an alternative form of masculinity emerges in which vulnerability is not a gendered feminine construct. For Koby, vulnerability can play a transformational role in navigating the complexities of relationships and Israeli society.

The new masculinity that emerges for Koby is one that embodies elements from both masculine and feminine hegemony. By creating characters who each possess traits of hegemonic masculinity *and* femininity like Koby and Numi, Modan is envisioning an alternate gendered space within Israeli society. This new space shatters the strict dichotomy between gendered roles and instead prioritizes other, more salient features, like confidence, vulnerability, and compassion. The two protagonists' willingness to become vulnerable with each other by acknowledging their own weaknesses and limitations facilitates an ability to connect with each other. Koby's type of masculinity has been called the "empathic man", and it has begun gaining traction among Israeli youth but still lags far behind the hegemonic model in making a noticeable impact on shaping Israeli society.[22] Within the text and in Israeli society, it is still manly men and effeminate women who are revered. For Modan, however, Gabriel's hypermasculinity is to be criticized for the emotional toil it wreaks on his family. Instead, like Dana Olmert's contention that Israeli literary writers have begun challenging hegemonic femininity with regards to the role that mothers have while waiting for their sons to return from battle,[23] I contend that by prominently featuring Koby, a male who in his manliness comes to apologize and to recognize his mistakes, Modan is articulating an alternative vision for masculinity within Israeli society.

Sensitivity in the necropolis in Etgar Keret and Asaf Hanuka's *Pizzeria Kamikaze*

Etgar Keret and Asaf Hanuka's *Pizzeria Kamikaze* was first written by Keret and published by Zmora Bitan in 1998 as a short story called "Kneller's Happy Campers" before being released as a graphic novel illustrated by Hanuka in 2004 and reissued in 2018 by Archaia. Like the original short story, *Pizzeria Kamikaze* was published in Hebrew before being translated into English.[24] *Pizzeria Kamikaze* is not Keret's first story to be turned into a graphic novel, as a number of graphic novel adaptations of Keret's work have been produced by Actus Tragicus as part of a previously released work entitled *Jetlag*. Keret's works lend themselves to visualization, as his post-modern short stories include many fantastical elements that call out for illustration, as well as having few and spare details, which frees artists to create their own interpretations of his words. *Pizzeria Kamikaze* is set in a Tel Aviv-like necropolis populated by people who died by suicide. The primary storyline revolves around a character named Mordy who struggles to form emotional bonds with the people around him. The story begins after Mordy has already died by suicide following the dissolution of his relationship with his girlfriend Desiree. In the afterlife, Mordy works at a pizza shop called *Pizzeria Kamikaze* and spends time with his friend Uzi, who died by suicide by shooting himself in the face. Mordy learns that Desiree also died by suicide and decides that he must find her so that they can rekindle their romance in the necropolis. As Mordy searches for her, he develops feelings for a troubled woman named Leehee, who is convinced that she did not die by suicide and has been incorrectly placed in the necropolis for suicides. Eventually, just as Leehee is taken away by a committee that determined that she was correct, Mordy realizes that he no longer loves Desiree and that he loves Leehee instead. The text concludes much like it began, with Mordy waiting and pining for a girl that he loves who no longer exists in his world.

As Keret is one of Israel's most prominent writers, his original short story and the graphic novel adaptation have received scholarly attention. Harris has argued that the story is a critique on the ways that the city of Tel Aviv has come to be revered within Israeli society and Israeli literature as a metonym of the new Israeli Jew who would be different from the European Jew. She writes: "Tel Aviv was intended to be an architectural manifestation of this newness" but the city has come to represent the "failure of the Zionist dream" and "the annihilation and corruption of the society that remains".[25] Setting Tel Aviv as the site for where all people who die by suicide gather, suggests Harris, reflects a vision of the Zionist enterprise in shambles, collapsing under its own weight. Ariel Kahn has argued that *Pizzeria Kamikaze* is a critique of military heroization; the illusion that soldiers make noble sacrifices for the state and are rewarded for their bravery is undermined by celebrating a culture of death in the afterlife.[26]

Like Harris' contention that converting Tel Aviv into a necropolis subverts hegemonic attitudes about Israeli culture and society, the heroization of a character who died by suicide is also a critique against hegemonic notions of masculinity. Harris correctly notes that suicide as a literary trope needs to be considered within its cultural context.[27] As I noted in the introduction, soldiers who die fighting bravely in defense of Israel are heroic and therefore masculine. Dying by suicide is therefore the antithesis of masculinity, and Mordy's decision to terminate his life over a broken heart and to capitulate to his feelings of despair and depression runs counter to notions of manliness. Throughout *Pizzeria Kamikaze*, the characters refer to "Juliets", women who die by suicide in ways that do not mar their bodies and preserve their beauty. The text makes no mention of men who die by suicide like this, nor is Mordy ever called a Juliet despite dying by suicide in a way that leaves no visible mark on his body. Mordy's suicide contrasts with that of his friend Uzi, who shot himself in the head and who is depicted with a large hole in his face that has accompanied him to the afterlife. If Mordy's decision to die by suicide is itself a non-masculine performative act, his subsequent decision to do so in a way that did not hurt or visibly scar his body further distances him from more hegemonic masculine behaviors.

Despite dying by suicide like a Juliet, Mordy is not identified within the text as a feminine character. Instead, like Modan did in *Exit Wounds* with Koby, Keret and Hanuka use Mordy to serve as a critique of the ways that masculinity has come to be defined in Israeli society. Nurit Buchweitz has suggested that creating male characters who *appear* to be heteronormative Israelis but challenge or subvert that heteronormativity is a hallmark of Keret's writing.[28] In a society that prizes men for their bravery, heroism, and ability to stand out, Mordy's masculinity is evident in more subtle and genuine ways that reflect the complexities and nuances of daily life. This is most clear in the ways that Mordy thoughtfully and methodically remains consistent in his core personality. Throughout the story Mordy is a quiet character; at the beginning of the text Mordy is also depressed. However, as Mordy becomes more involved with Leehee, his depression fades and his personality as a reflective individual remains. Mordy's masculinity, while shrouded in silences, is supportive to Leehee, even though he knows this will result in her no longer being present in the necropolis. In the final scene of the graphic novel, Mordy hangs a sign upside down on the door of Pizzeria Kamikaze; this subtle action is a reference to a conversation that he and Leehee had earlier in their relationship. It is designed to help Leehee find him again in the future and to allow her to feel comfortable in her new space.

While Mordy both begins and ends the graphic novel hoping to reconnect with a lost love, his attitude towards the women has shifted, as has his own expression of masculinity. Throughout *Pizzeria Kamikaze*, Mordy's friend Uzi repeatedly encourages him to assume greater signifiers of hegemonic Israeli masculinity; he discourages Mordy from socializing with Arabs, he encourages Mordy to have sex with random women, he complains when Mordy does not want to go drinking and partying. Uzi is a member of "a distinct sector of Israeli society – young people who roam from one bar to another in search of incidental company [and] share apartments with partners that they do not really like".[29] Throughout the work, Mordy resists Uzi's pressure, not succumbing to this brand of masculinity. Instead, Mordy remains consistent in wanting to be in a committed relationship, but he comes to better understand that his relationship with Desiree was superficial, unlike his relationship with Leehee wherein they had more meaningful conversations about the purpose of life.

Through these conversations, Mordy realizes that his own life has meaning and purpose and that he wants to have friendships and relationships in the necropolis.[30] Kahn traces this realization to Leehee's impact on his development as a character.[31] Physiognomically, this shift is depicted in subtle ways. Prior to meeting Leehee, Mordy is often illustrated slouched over with his hair matted down and he is always clothed; once his relationship develops with Leehee, his posture changes, as does his hair. He now stands upright and fashionably styles his hair. As well, the reader comes to learn that Mordy possesses a chiseled yet lean physique, one that mirrors the desired Israeli masculine body (Figure 1.4). By hiding Mordy's body and denying him access to hegemonic visual signifiers until after he demonstrates a changed personality, Keret and Hanuka diminish the value of physique in relation to masculinity, personality, and behavior. It is the mind and not the body of the man that determines masculinity, and by not allowing the reader to know about Mordy's body until late in the text, the reader is forced to first consider Mordy's personality rather than his physique.

Alongside his physical transformation, what most significantly emerges is a shift in how Mordy shares his personality and the ways that other characters come to respect his non-hegemonic masculinity. Kahn writes that Leehee "has transformed Mordy into a different kind of hero, one who acts playfully rather than violently".[32] Mordy's playfulness reflects a different type of masculinity and is one that values the interpersonal dynamic that can exist between two people. At one point in *Pizzeria Kamikaze*, Mordy is frustrated that he is not like some of the other characters, who are able to perform fantastical magic tricks. His frustration ebbs when he comes to accept that he needs to be who he is and to not try to pass as someone that he is not, even if this means being

Figure 1.4 Mordy displaying a hegemonically Israeli masculine physique.
Credit: Etgar Keret and Asaf Hanuka, *Pizzeria Kamikaze*
(Los Angeles: Archaia, 2018).

different from the people around him. De-emphasizing the bombastic and bloated masculinity that has characterized Israeli society leads to the development of a character that is not weak, but humble and confident in his own quirkiness as he comes to accept parts of himself that might be at odds with those around him who perform hegemonic masculinity. Roman Katsman writes that a tenet of Keret's work involves considering "the ability to live out the profound problems without ever repressing them and without aching them or scorning them, without trying fervently to solve them".[33] Mordy's is a masculinity that is open to flexibility, complexity, instability, and confusion and that does not require objective gendered delineations to demarcate spaces and identities. It is a masculinity that is thoughtfully and purposefully monogamous and which values intimate dialogue before physical intimacy. Significantly, by the end of the graphic novel, it is Uzi's hypermasculinity that has faded, since he not only chooses to enter a committed relationship with a girl that he meets, but refuses to return to the bustling necropolis, preferring to reside in the countryside. Unlike Uzi's masculinity, which was transient, superficial, and ultimately weak in impact, it is Mordy's more genuine and subtle approach to masculinity that has an impact on the characters around him and which suggests a way out of the dangerous hegemonic masculinity that has come to define Israeli society.

Mizrahi manliness in Asaf Hanuka's "The Realist"

Asaf Hanuka began publishing his weekly editorial cartoon "The Realist" in *Calcalist* in 2010. As an Israeli business magazine, *Calcalist* reports on local and international economic affairs, but its target audience is the average Israeli and not one who is an economist.[34] Asaf Hanuka's "The Realist" comfortably fits into the paper's ethos, as he represents the voice of the average Israeli who needs to work within the economy even though he is not an expert about the economy. Unlike the fictional *Exit Wounds* and *Pizzeria Kamikaze*, "The Realist" is a work of non-fiction that introduces the reader to the real-life experiences of Hanuka and his family. Each weekly installment of the series is a self-contained comic, and while the characters repeat from week to week, a new story or event in their lives is told each time. A number of the strips have been collected and published by Archaia in volumes issued in 2015 and 2017.

Hanuka's own Israeli story is one that diverges from the hegemonic masculine Israeli narrative. He is the child of Mizrahi, or Judeo-Arab, parents and therefore grew up in the pale of Mizrahi gender norms. These norms operate differently from hegemonic Israeli gender norms, but given the prominent place of Ashkenazi culture and history in Israeli society and its school curriculum, Hanuka would certainly have been aware of normative Ashkenazi gender constructs. Unlike the Ashkenazi gender norms that Israelis eschewed, Mizrahi physical attributes tend to favor hypermasculinity and were therefore revered by Jewish Israelis.[35] Despite the estimation for the Mizrahi body, the Israeli patriarchy viewed Mizrahim as uncultured and retrograde because they came from societies that were culturally different European ones.[36] Mizrahim were often at a cultural disadvantage within Israeli society.[37] A further difference between Hanuka and the hegemonic Israeli man is that he did not serve in an elite army unit; instead, he worked in a non-combat role by staffing the military's weekly newspaper as an illustrator and graphic artist.

Within "The Realist", Hanuka's illustrative style is hyperrealistic. Facial features, bodily physiognomy and hair (or lack of hair) are all illustrated in rich detail. Hanuka does not obfuscate his own body's flaws; he illustrates himself as he is, not presenting himself in an inauthentic way. This includes illustrating hairy arms and legs, a bald head, and a paunch at his belly. Realistic depictions of this nature serve to simultan-eously connote to the reader elements of honesty while also introducing alternative depictions of masculinity. Visualizations of the very ordin-ariness of Hanuka's body alongside honest depictions of what happens to the male body as it ages force the reader to be confronted with evidence of the limitations of hegemonic masculinity. Unlike a text-only work, where the reader's imagination creates the visualization, a comic provides no room for the reader to evade the reality that Hanuka is depicting, which is that not every man in Israel possesses the chiseled and toned hegemonic body, especially once they enter their forties, like Hanuka has.

In a comic entitled "Statistical Distribution" (Figure 1.5), Hanuka illustrated himself as a nearly naked dismembered body. Like a pie chart, Hanuka labels five areas around his body with titles, percentages, and explanations. Hanuka labels both "Jewish Israeli" and "Mizrahi" as 100 per cent. Under Mizrahi, he traces his family's ancestry in the Middle East. Under Jewish Israeli, Hanuka writes he was "cut into at 8 days of age" – a reference to his ritual circumcision as a Jew – and he has "a title in the state-issued ID card", which identifies him as a Jew and a citizen of Israel.[38] Hanuka illustrates these aspects of his identity as disjointed and not part of a cohesive whole, particularly his separation of his Mizrahi and Jewish identities. The physical separation of his body parts also reflects a lack of coherence and self-perception of belonging within Israel as an integrated citizen. His identification as both 100 per cent Mizrahi and Jewish Israeli, yet his choice to leave them as separate aspects of himself, suggests incompatibility, as evidenced by the autopsy he has performed upon himself. Despite living in the Jewish homeland, Hanuka still feels like an outsider as a Mizrahi man living in Israel. Tahneer Oksman writes, "Many Jewish women cartoonists have embraced an autobiographical approach to the medium partly to project their own fantasies and anxieties about what it means to be an outsider within one's assigned community".[39] Notwithstanding the gen-dered dynamic in her analysis, this statement might apply equally to Hanuka's anxieties as a Mizrahi male, as well as his place as an adult who wants Israeli society to be different from what it presently is.

In addition to interrogating normative constructions of mascu-linity by realistically illustrating his body, Hanuka also challenges these constructs based on how he depicts his relationships with his wife and with his children. In a number of his comics, he illustrates how he is a flawed and imperfect partner with his wife. These imperfections include not listening to her when she speaks to him, expecting that she bear a greater household responsibility than he does, and being more engrossed

STATISTICAL DISTRIBUTION

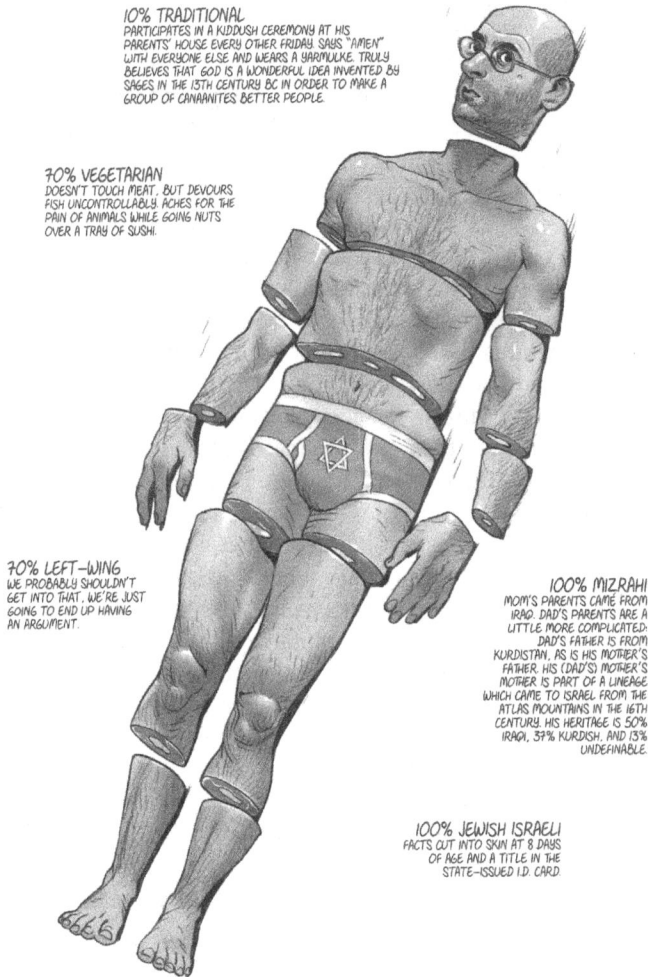

10% TRADITIONAL
PARTICIPATES IN A KIDDUSH CEREMONY AT HIS
PARENTS' HOUSE EVERY OTHER FRIDAY. SAYS "AMEN"
WITH EVERYONE ELSE AND WEARS A YARMULKE. TRULY
BELIEVES THAT GOD IS A WONDERFUL IDEA INVENTED BY
SAGES IN THE 15TH CENTURY BC IN ORDER TO MAKE A
GROUP OF CANAANITES BETTER PEOPLE.

70% VEGETARIAN
DOESN'T TOUCH MEAT, BUT DEVOURS
FISH UNCONTROLLABLY. ACHES FOR THE
PAIN OF ANIMALS WHILE GOING NUTS
OVER A TRAY OF SUSHI.

70% LEFT-WING
WE PROBABLY SHOULDN'T
GET INTO THAT. WE'RE JUST
GOING TO END UP HAVING
AN ARGUMENT.

100% MIZRAHI
MOM'S PARENTS CAME FROM
IRAQ. DAD'S PARENTS ARE A
LITTLE MORE COMPLICATED:
DAD'S FATHER IS FROM
KURDISTAN, AS IS HIS MOTHER'S
FATHER. HIS (DAD'S) MOTHER'S
MOTHER IS PART OF A LINEAGE
WHICH CAME TO ISRAEL FROM THE
ATLAS MOUNTAINS IN THE 16TH
CENTURY. HIS HERITAGE IS 50%
IRAQI, 37% KURDISH, AND 13%
UNDEFINABLE.

100% JEWISH ISRAELI
FACTS CUT INTO SKIN AT 8 DAYS
OF AGE AND A TITLE IN THE
STATE-ISSUED I.D. CARD.

Figure 1.5 Asaf Hanuka dismembers his body and identity. Credit: Asaf
Hanuka, "Statistical Distribution," *The Realist: Plug and Play*
(Los Angeles: Archaia, 2017).

in his cell phone than in talking to her. In "Of Course I'm Listening", Hanuka illustrates himself in conversation with his wife in outer space. She is emotional and is hiding her face while crying into her hands. Seated opposite her at the table is Hanuka, wearing a full space suit. The space suit symbolizes a barrier that prevents Hanuka from being emotionally connected to his wife in her moment of distress and results in their being isolated from each other even as they share the same physical space. Comics like "Of Course I'm Listening" and many others paint an unflattering portrait of Hanuka and the way that he treats his wife. Yet it is their very realness which points a finger at the way that men behave in general and calls for alternative ways of interacting with women. In comics like these, Hanuka is not portraying himself as a villain but as a real person who behaves imperfectly in his marriage. By calling attention to his own flaws as a husband and partner, Hanuka similarly calls attention to the flaws of other men, and through this heightened awareness, he identifies a need to become a kinder and more attentive partner. Acknowledging a masculinity of this nature departs from the normative by recognizing the need to establish a masculinity that is sensitive and attuned to the emotional needs of one's partner.

When illustrating comics with his children, a common theme that Hanuka frequently addresses is his own vulnerability in relation to them. He is both aware and willing to share that when he leaves his children for the day it makes him sad and that when he works hard all day his emotional outlet is being able to spend time with his children when he returns home. In "Brave Heart" Hanuka illustrates himself crying after saying goodbye to his children. This depiction of a vulnerable man who cries over being separated from his children is not the macho and tough Israeli who isolates himself from his emotions and is nonplussed by separating from his children. Instead, this is a father who is so comfortable and confident with his feelings that he is willing to depict a natural human reaction that many parents feel when they drop their children off at daycare in the morning. A further way that Hanuka challenges normative masculinity is by demonstrating how he has adopted elements of normative femininity with how he relates to his family. In a comic entitled "Deadlines", Hanuka illustrates himself dressed in a karate outfit, battling against ninjas and assassins who attack him as he tries to return home (Figure 1.6). Throughout the first eight panels of the strip, Hanuka is bloody and beaten and visibly exhausted from what he has experienced throughout the day. In the final panel, Hanuka is playing happily with his son. Whereas hegemonic masculinity in Israeli society emphasizes the husband's success and acclaim based on what he accomplishes outside of the home, here, by envisioning the tropes of

Figure 1.6 Asaf Hanuka fights enemies in order to spend time with his family. Credit: Asaf Hanuka, "Deadlines," The Realist (Los Angeles: Archaia, 2015).

masculinity anew, Hanuka adopts elements of hegemonic femininity by illustrating how all of his toils are so that he can enjoy and benefit from what happens inside his home.

A common thread that runs through Hanuka's observations about his own masculinity is irony. He regularly calls attention to the ways that men think they are behaving heroically when in fact they are not. Hanuka accomplishes this by illustrating himself costumed as Superman while performing mundane and routine tasks. In "Burp Man", Hanuka is seen flying through the air, burping his infant daughter, and in "Handy Man", he is hanging a mirror in his home and sees himself as Superman in the reflection while his wife nervously looks on, oblivious to Hanuka's self-assessment of himself as Superman. The juxtaposition of seeing himself as Superman – a paragon of masculinity – while performing everyday chores around the house destabilizes notions of masculinity. The use of the Superman motif allows Hanuka to cleverly contrast the ways that he wishes his wife would see him in relation to the way that he sees himself. In a further ironic twist, in 2017 Hanuka issued a new comic called "Local Wonder"; in it, his wife was illustrated cleaning a window as he nervously stood by spotting for her, and in her reflection in the window, Hanuka illustrated Wonder Woman. Just like in Handy Man, when it was only Hanuka who saw himself as Superman and not his wife, here, too, it is only Hanuka who sees Wonder Woman in the reflection. By reversing the performative roles but retaining who sees the superhero, Hanuka suggests that he sees his wife as a superhero who mightily solves the family's messiest problems. Seeing both himself and his wife as a superhero establishes a balance between how he understands his wife's importance and role within their relationship. When considered alongside "Handy Man" and "Burp Man", "Local Wonder" suggests that both play crucial roles inside and outside the home and that the performance of these tasks strengthens the familial unit.

Asaf Hanuka's depictions of masculinity are similar to the type of masculinity that Orna Sasson-Levy has termed "home-based masculinity".[40] Found primarily in men who are not Ashkenazi and who did not serve in combat units in the army – both of which are descriptors of Hanuka – adherents to home-based masculinity "accentuate the importance of home and family … [and] emphasize autonomy, independence, and responsibility in the private sphere".[41] For these men, their relationships with their families supersede their national duties, and it is at home where they are most able to demonstrate their masculinity by being caregivers and providers for their family members. Throughout "The Realist", Hanuka's emphasis on his family and the ways that he frames his worldly responsibilities in relation to his familial responsibilities reflect an adoption of this non-hegemonic Israeli masculinity. The significance of Hanuka's willingness to produce and publish hundreds of comics that introduce and reify home-based masculinity cannot be understated. *Calcalist*'s print and online readership totals over 2.7 million readers,[42] and this does not include the readers who get to see every comic on Hanuka's Facebook page or the readers of the collected editions of "The Realist" that have been published in many languages. Unlike individual novels or texts that introduce an idea but are then maybe forgotten over time, the repetitive nature of Hanuka's depictions of the minutiae of his familial experiences allows them to serve as disrupters to the entropic process that naturally occurs when defaulting to foundational myths. While certainly not bombastic or loud, the monotony of ten years of comics that challenge hegemonic narratives ensures that the message does not fade over time; instead, by returning again and again to depictions of home-based masculinity, Hanuka facilitates opportunities for regularly challenging the ways that Israeli society remains tethered to hegemonic masculinities.

As a visual medium that is still emerging within Israeli society, comics and graphic novels are able to advance narratives and ideologies that diverge from the normative constructs while operating under the radar of scrutiny. The texts considered here provide readers with opportunities not only to *read* but to *see* men in action. These men perform gender in new ways, and this type of reconceptualization of Israeli gender is standard practice in Israeli graphic novels. Despite Marjorie C. Allison's contention that Rutu Modan's *Exit Wounds* "reveals a type of narrative that has been marginalized and excluded from mainstream literatures",[43] this is not the case within the Israeli milieu. Narratives that challenge the hegemony like Modan's might be outliers in the American corpus, but they are the norm within Israeli comics culture. It is the message of graphic novels by writers like Modan, Folman, Hanuka, and Keret that have been marginalized in *Israeli society*. Works like these, however, can serve as models for shifting the ways that masculinity is constructed in Israeli society. The visual stimuli across all four texts allow readers to step into the characters' homes, cars, and businesses, and to see how they live their daily lives and interact with the people around them. Being able to see what the characters wear on a daily basis, how they style their hair, and how they perform masculinity in a visual media is far more immersive than the experience provided by literary works because of the visual signifiers that are included in every panel.

The texts analyzed in this chapter all recognize aspects of the Israeli hegemonic masculine ideal and then work to subvert it by replacing it with different forms of masculinity. The alternative expressions – while different for each text – acknowledge that not all Israeli men fit the hegemonic model and, more importantly, that this model might not best serve the interests of Israeli society. Changing a society – even one as young as Israel's – is no simple feat. Perhaps what can be learned by analyzing these four texts together is a need to begin the process. Together, Modan, Keret, Folman, Polonsky, and Hanuka advocate for alternative masculinities that move beyond the reactionary gendered constructs that were established in the formative years of the state and which have come to define it. What *Waltz with Bashir*, *Exit Wounds*, *Pizzeria Kamikaze* and "The Realist" effectively accomplish is that they not only show the ineffectiveness of the hegemonic model but offer examples for different types of men who can populate Israeli society and contribute to it as valued men. This masculinity is one that is more in touch with emotions and feelings; it is a masculinity that is fluid and adaptive; it is a masculinity that responds to the needs of others. It is one that consistently emphasizes vulnerability as a necessary trait for interacting with the world. It is a masculinity that less needs to prove itself and instead is at home and comfortable with itself. This masculinity recognizes that before one can heal the state, one first needs to heal oneself and, through that process, become a better man who is able to be a part of society as well.

Notes

1 Hanuka's work on "The Realist" has been published online at www.calcalist. co.il and on social media sites like Facebook and Instagram and has been translated into numerous languages and published in collected volumes. As of publication, two English-languages volumes have been released, and these two are the primary texts used when analyzing Hanuka's comics in this chapter and in the following chapter. See Hanuka, *The Realist* and Hanuka, *The Realist: Plug and Play*.
2 Munk, "From National Heroes", 312.
3 Harris, *Warriors, Witches, Whores*.
4 Hollander, "Shifting Manhood", 348.
5 Hollander, "Shifting Manhood", 348.
6 Folman and Polonsky, *Waltz with Bashir*, 6.
7 Folman and Polonsky, *Waltz with Bashir*, 20.
8 Folman and Polonsky, *Waltz with Bashir*, 44.
9 Folman and Polonsky, *Waltz with Bashir*, 20.
10 Hollander, "Shifting Manhood", 357.
11 Modan, "Jamilti".
12 Modan, "Homecoming".

13 Olmert, "Mothers of Soldiers", 341–342.
14 Levy, Hollander and Noy-Canyon, "The Construction", 550.
15 Levy, Hollander and Noy-Canyon, "The Construction", 564.
16 Haworth, *The Comics of Rutu Modan*, 67.
17 Haworth, *The Comics of Rutu Modan*, 70.
18 Sion and Ben-Ari, "Imagined Masculinity", 21.
19 Sion and Ben-Ari, "Imagined Masculinity", 37.
20 Modan, *Exit Wounds*, 86.
21 Tabachnick, "Strange Encounters", 232.
22 Levy, Hollander and Noy-Canyon, "The Construction", 552.
23 Olmert, "Mothers of Soldiers", 347.
24 Some character names differ between the English and Hebrew versions and between the short story and the graphic novel versions. For the purposes of clarity, and since names and the distinctions between the texts are not the focus of this chapter, all references to the story are to the names and identifying features found in the English edition of the graphic novel *Pizzeria Kamikaze*.
25 Harris, *An Ideological Death*, 169.
26 Kahn, "From Darkness into Light", 205.
27 Harris, *An Ideological Death*, 211.
28 Buchweitz, "Vitalities and Fatalities", 40.
29 Weissbrod and Kohn, "Collaborative Self-Translation", 411.
30 Harris, "Decay and Death", 90.
31 Kahn, "From Darkness into Light", 209.
32 Kahn, "From Darkness into Light", 210.
33 Katsman, "Ishiyut, Etika ve-Ideologiya", 32.
34 Esteron, Hemi and Kessler, "About Calcalist".
35 Hirsch and Grosswirth Kachtan, "Is 'Hegemonic Masculinity'", 688.
36 Hirsch and Grosswirth Kachtan, "Is 'Hegemonic Masculinity'", 691.
37 Hirsch and Grosswirth Kachtan, "Is 'Hegemonic Masculinity'", 690.
38 Hanuka, *The Realist: Plug and Play*.
39 Oksman, *How Come Boys*, 18.
40 Sasson-Levy, "Military, Masculinity, and Citizenship", 320.
41 Sasson-Levy, "Military, Masculinity, and Citizenship", 320.
42 *Calcalist*, "Who is the Big Winner".
43 Allison, "(Not) Lost", 87.

2 Outspoken and adventurous women in Israeli graphic novels

Matt Reingold

Like Israeli graphic novels that challenge traditional notions of masculinity, a similar type of expression has been presented with regards to femininity in Israeli graphic novels as well. Artists and writers depict a femininity that is not solely tied either to the military or to motherhood. While the military is inescapable in Israeli society, in the graphic novels that will be considered in this chapter, it does not serve as the fulcrum that defines the way the female characters express their gendered identities. Instead, Israeli graphic novels offer alternative constructions of how femininity can be performed within Israeli society, arguing for a more expansive and complex understanding of the ways that women identify with their gender and interact with both men and women in Israeli society.

The texts that I will be using to explore representations of femininity are two of the short stories contained in Galit and Gilad Seliktar's *Farm 54*, Rutu Modan's Eisner-award winning graphic novel *The Property* and Asaf Hanuka's previously analyzed weekly series "The Realist". *Farm 54* is a collection of three short stories set in the years between the First Lebanon War in 1982 and the beginning of First Palestinian Intifada in 1989. The basis of the three stories are Galit's autobiographical experiences growing up in a rural community in Israel, but she embellishes and fictionalizes plot points in all three. The first story, entitled "Substitute Lifeguard", is a coming-of-age story in which a teenager named Noga is so focused on kissing a boy in a swimming pool that she does not realize that her baby brother has drowned nearby in the pool. In "Houses", the Seliktars tell a story with two parts: in the first, Noga's friendship with a Palestinian is questioned by a co-worker who assumes an undesired maternal role in Noga's life, while in the second, Noga is forced to bear witness while Israeli soldiers destroy a Palestinian home. Like the previously considered Numi in *Exit Wounds*, Modan's *The Property* features a strong female character in Mica, the

DOI: 10.4324/9781003150435-3

granddaughter of Holocaust survivor Regina. Unlike the former text, *The Property* is primarily set in Poland, as Mica and Regina travel to Warsaw purportedly to reclaim their family's pre-war property. And finally, I will return to Hanuka's "The Realist", but my focus will shift from Hanuka's autobiographical exploration of his own masculinity and instead turn to how he depicts his wife Hilit.

Erotic desire and Arab friendship in Galit and Gilad Seliktar's *Farm 54*

Originally released in French before being translated into English and published by Fanfare/Ponent Mon in 2011, Galit and Gilad Seliktar's *Farm 54* is a collection of three short stories set over an eight-year period between 1981 and 1989. The stories were originally written by Galit, a published author, as short prose pieces, before being illustrated by her brother Gilad, an instructor at Bezalel Academy of Art and Design. *Farm 54* is a semi-autobiographical text whose setting is inspired by Ganei-Yohanan, a rural agricultural community in Israel where the siblings grew up. The main character of *Farm 54* is Noga, a young Israeli girl who lives in a fictional version of Ganei-Yohanan in the geographic center of the country. Across the three stories, the reader comes to meet Noga's family at three seminal moments in her life as she begins to feel empowered in her sexuality and challenged by her role in Israel's military establishment.

The text's first story, entitled "The Substitute Lifeguard", is narrated in first person by Noga as she chronicles what happens on the day that her younger brother Amnon drowns in a swimming pool. While not directly responsible for his death or for supervising him, Noga was kissing a boy in the pool at the time that Amnon drowned, and she was therefore present for his death. In the passages before Amnon's death, Noga describes the way that she subtly and coquettishly flirts with Dror, a boy who has repeatedly asked her to be his girlfriend, and to whom she had previously demurred. While initially reticent on that day too, she comes to appreciate the way that he sits poolside, "seeing only [her], alone among all those bobbing heads".[1] Once the pool has cleared out for lunchtime, Noga remains in the pool with Dror as she realizes that she is curious whether he will get an erection if they swim sensually together. As the two whisper in each other's ears, Noga shares with the reader how Dror's "underpants got really tight … and when he came close to me, [she] almost drowned from all the pleasantness and dizziness. A strange hunger overcame [her]. [She] bit Dror on the lips and couldn't stop".[2] Gilad's artwork is intensely minimalistic; most pages include three wide-frame panels that tell their own story, often with sparse details. Employing only black for lines and shading and an earthy mauve-like color for shadowing in some spaces, the reader is given tremendous responsibility to construct meaning. Working like a film director, Gilad carefully draws the reader in to the swimming pool where Noga assumes responsibility for orchestrating her moment of intimacy. As Noga becomes more and more interested in exploring what would happen to Dror if she lets him come closer to her, Gilad carefully focuses the reader's attention on the micro-details of physical intimacy while simultaneously allowing the reader's imagination to fill in some of the gaps. As Noga describes how Dror touched her face while holding on to the side of the pool, Gilad illustrates a hand holding the side of the pool, leaving the reader's imagination free to visualize what that looks like. Next, the reader sees Dror's nose and lips, whispering into Noga's ear. Then, two parted lips are illustrated but the kiss itself is not depicted (Figure 2.1). The juxtaposition of closeups of disembodied body parts with the slow burn of descriptively heightened sexuality creates an intensely personal experience as the reader comes to assume a voyeuristic position in Noga's sexual awakening.

Dror is not a boy that Noga has just met; he is someone she has known and who has expressed erotic feelings for her. And yet she makes it clear to the reader that she did not suddenly capitulate to his desire, caving in under the pressure and weight of his interest. As depicted in the text, Dror places no pressure on Noga; even as he expresses love for her, he does not physically actualize intimacy until Noga uses her body to convey desire to him. The Seliktars' linguistic and artistic depictions of Noga's burgeoning sexuality introduce to the reader a character who is coming to better understand not only her own erotic desires and curiosity, but the ways that her eroticism affects others. She does not want to see Dror's penis; instead, she wants to see how her behavior causes a reaction from Dror's penis. Noga's focus is on herself and the ways that her femininity can be used in relation to men and not on the male body in and of itself. Noga's awareness of how she caused Dror's erection leads her to become even more confident, initiating the kiss that will soon come to be associated with death. Noga's sexual empowerment operates in contrast to a traditional understanding that in Israel, "women's wants and desires were considered bourgeois and had no place in the creation of the nation".[3] It is only in films produced in recent decades – and primarily in those directed by women – where women experience sexual and personal liberty on their own terms and with how "they display sexual interest and sexual availability".[4] Referencing Maya Dreifuss' film *She's Coming Home*, Rachel S. Harris identifies that its significance revolves

His underpants got really tight like the sub's and, when he came close to me, I almost drowned from all the pleasantness and dizziness.

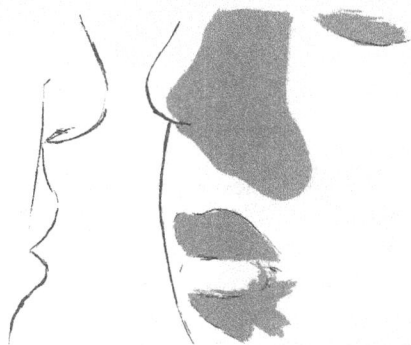

A strange hunger overcame me.

Figure 2.1 Sexual intimacy between Noga and Dror. Credit: Galit Seliktar and Gilad Seliktar, *Farm 54* (Wisbech, England: Fanfare/Ponent Mon, 2011).

around its characterization of a woman who decides to not remain attached to vestiges of a femininity that no longer reflect her identity.[5] Similarly, in *Farm 54*, Noga's decision to initiate her sexual relationship with Dror involves her own rejection of gendered notions that subsume women's sexual identities beneath those of the men around them, and are instead reflective of an increased presence within Israeli literature and film of empowered female characters who do not remain tethered to hegemonic femininity.

Noga's moment of intimacy is interrupted with the tragedy of her brother's very preventable death a few feet away from her. While Noga is navigating her feelings as a sensual and sexual woman, she is oblivious to the death of her brother right beside her. Even as her mother is screaming for Amnon, Noga remains focused on Dror and their first kiss. Josh Lambert has noted how Gilad does not depict the search for Amnon; instead, Gilad illustrates the inside of the family's home, creating an effect which is "unexpected and chilling, a sharp evocation of that feeling of eerie disembodiment that occurs in the first moments of a panic".[6] Unnarrated, Noga and Dror stare at Amnon in the pool, frozen in place, unable to move to save him. Accompanying the image is a description of who does jump into the pool: "Dad ran to the edge of the pool and, just before he jumped, we saw Amnon right next to us floating in the calm water".[7] As she comes to experience sexual gratification, Noga performs femininity in a way that is different from the trope of Israeli literary femininity. She is a sexual being and not the maternal figure who protects and guards over children. While obviously Amnon's sister and not his mother, Noga's focus throughout the scene remains on Dror, a boy outside of her family, and not on hearing her own mother's voice or being aware of her father's panicked presence. And yet I do not see in this break from hegemonic Israeli femininity a critique of Noga's alternative femininity or a suggestion that the hegemony should be maintained, nor do I see a claim that feminine sexuality be correlated with loss. Instead, I see a recognition that femininity is a highly contested and complex space with multiple competing sites and that space needs to be carved out for Israeli women to embrace their sexual autonomy and lived independence without having to simultaneously sacrifice familial responsibilities. Noga's inability to do so because of the ways that hegemonic femininity are impressed upon her ultimately lead to tragedy.

The duality of sexual inclination alongside familial or national responsibilities is a complex dichotomy that comes to also factor into "Houses", the third story of *Farm 54*. Like "The Substitute Lifeguard", which has two interconnected storylines, "Houses" similarly juxtaposes two autobiographical events from Galit's life, told through the voice of the fictional character Noga. The first revolves around a day shortly before Noga enlists in the IDF while working at an egg farm. There, she has become friends with a Palestinian man named As'ad. The two casually chat while they work and, on her last day working at the farm, As'ad gifts her with a cassette tape of Arabic music for her to listen to while on duty in the army. The second event takes place on her first night in the IDF. Assigned to an education department in the West Bank, Noga is asked to accompany a troop of excited soldiers as they searched, evacuated, and demolished an Arab home near Bethlehem. Noga attends the demolition, but she does not take part in any of the violence or destruction. She remains a bystander, uncomfortably accepting the words of her fellow soldier who says: "They don't demolish houses for no reason".[8]

In the first part of the story where she befriends As'ad, Noga reveals to the reader that, despite her playful workplace banter, she has a boyfriend who she sees on the weekends when he is on leave from his duties as an IDF soldier. Whether Noga or As'ad have sexual desire for each other is never addressed in the story, but what is evident is that the two have a nice and comfortable friendship. As'ad jokes with Noga about what happens to the eggs that break (they get turned into candies for children), he is supportive of her enlistment (even though he is Palestinian), and he prepares her a mixtape of Arabic music to listen to while she is in the army. Noga's friendship with As'ad upsets Tamara, the egg factory's forewoman, and leads her to subtly criticize Noga. In one scene, Tamara remarks to Noga how "it seems that this As'ad is getting too friendly with you…"[9], while in another she questions whether Noga will take care of As'ad's Palestinian friends once she is in the army, sarcastically suggesting that Noga will be expected to treat Palestinians aggressively when she is a soldier. While only appearing in a few scenes, Tamara is a significant character in the story. Serving as a metonym for the hegemonic Israeli woman, she worries that Noga's friendship with As'ad is inappropriate for a Jewish Israeli young adult. Dating, let alone marrying and raising children with As'ad, is tantamount to treason within traditional Israeli femininity because it assumes that this relationship will weaken the collective Israeli community, and Tamara therefore works to preserve the hegemonic imperative by questioning Noga's motivations for being friendly with As'ad, discouraging her from even being his friend.

Noga's friendship with As'ad is indirectly called into question when she is forced to bear witness to a demolition of a Palestinian home. Initially assigned the role of instructor, a fellow female soldier claims she is having her period and asks if Noga can accompany a group of soldiers on a night-time mission. Reflecting Orlee Hauser's contention that women occupy a space in the army designed to manage and tame the men,[10] Noga is told that her role is to "follow the soldiers and make sure they don't touch the women when they evacuate the house",[11] and the male soldiers do not even provide her with a helmet to protect herself from debris. As opposed to participating in the mission – which she is told only happens for justified reasons – Noga is installed in a maternal role designed to protect the men from themselves in the event that they act out their hyperaggressive masculinity against Palestinian women.

Like Ari Folman and his troop of soldiers who provided lighting for the Phalangists to carry out the Sabra and Shatila massacre in *Waltz with Bashir* but did not enter the camp or physically attack Palestinians, Noga does not actually take part in the evacuation and demolition of the Palestinian home; instead, she stands, watching in silence as the male soldiers excitedly whoop and holler as they displace a Palestinian family from their home and their possessions. The story was rooted in an autobiographical experience, and Galit Seliktar has written about how she remains deeply troubled by her role as a bystander that night 20 years earlier. In the afterward to the story, she writes: "the night left its mark on me and for many years I repeatedly retold the events".[12]

I believe that Noga's friendship with As'ad explains why she was frozen in place during the operation, unable to process what she was witnessing. Chantal Catherine Michel identifies in Noga's relationship with As'ad a portrayal of Israelis and Arabs that is devoid of "stigmatizing and/or stereotyping".[13] Simply by being her friend, As'ad humanizes the Palestinian experience, forcing Noga to question the legitimacy of the soldiers' treatment of the Palestinian family. While rare in Israeli literature – and rarer still in real life – friendships and sexual relationships between Jewish women and Palestinian men invoke a challenge to the hegemonic gender structures that have been established in Israeli society. David C. Jacobson has argued that their existence in literature forces the reader to confront gender binaries and to consider the nature of the Israeli–Palestinian dichotomy and to what extent the barriers between the two peoples should remain fixed and in place. He notes:

> the very freedom of the writer to create an imagined fictional world allows for a refreshingly different set of possibilities than are typically actualized in real life ... These stories can be seen as "thought experiments" exploring the question of the potential and the limits of human intimacy between Israelis and Palestinians.[14]

For Noga, the contrast between As'ad's thoughtful kindness and the aggressive hypermasculinity of the soldiers leads her to being unable to reconcile her expected role of being a maternal figure with her revulsion at the Jewish-Israeli men's behavior. Galit's self-recrimination in the aftermath is a direct outcome of her belief that by silently serving her country and acquiescing to guard over the men it has produced as opposed to questioning the legitimacy of both the army and its soldiers, she failed a gendered test of her morality, and she manifests her trauma by needing to repeatedly tell her story. Doing so allows her to establish an alternate femininity, one that does not blindly follow the national narrative and one which questions the decisions made by its political institutions.

Independent women in Rutu Modan's *The Property*

Rutu Modan's[15] *The Property* was published in 2013 by Drawn & Quarterly, and like her earlier full-length graphic novel *Exit Wounds*, *The Property* was also recognized as the best graphic novel of the year at the Eisner Awards. Modan's story focuses on Holocaust survivor Regina Segal's trip to Warsaw with her granddaughter Mica after the death of Reuben, Regina's son and Mica's father. Regina plans the trip to Warsaw under the premise of taking possession of a family apartment that belonged to her parents before the outbreak of World War II. Even though the primary setting of the graphic novel is Warsaw, I have included it in this study because much of Mica's and Regina's behaviors and attitudes are shaped by their national identity as Israelis, and so the text is very much an Israeli graphic novel set in Poland. Shortly after arriving in Warsaw, Regina loses interest in reclaiming the property and becomes sullen and withdrawn. In an effort to find the apartment, Mica begins wandering around Warsaw, and she meets Tomasz Novak, a non-Jew who guides tourists on historical tours of Warsaw's Jewish neighborhoods. With Tomasz's help, Mica meets with a Polish lawyer and comes to learn that Poles did not illegally appropriate her family's property; in fact, it was sold by her great-grandparents before the war, and therefore, her family has no claim to it. The denouement of the text – and the real reason for the visit – emerges as the reader learns that Regina has been harboring a family secret. Before the Holocaust, she was in a romantic relationship with a non-Jewish Polish man named Roman Gorski. While with Roman, Regina became pregnant with Mica's father, and she was sent to Palestine by her parents in order to hide the pregnancy. In exchange for Roman's silence, he was sold the apartment by Regina's parents. Regina's return to Poland is not for reclaiming a property, but for reconnecting with Roman. This would allow her to become unburdened from the weight of hiding the fact that Mica's grandfather was a non-Jew and that Mica's father never even knew this. Shoshana Ronen has identified how narratives where Jews try to reclaim property from before the war typically end in tragedy and sadness. In *The Property*, however, "Modan turns it into a story of love, affection, and longing. Instead of fighting and hating one another, the Jews and Poles in the novel make love".[16]

Mica is a very different protagonist than Numi from *Exit Wounds*. Unlike Numi, who was described as awkward and shy, who was not regarded as beautiful by her own family, and who struggled to find anyone willing to help her determine Gabriel's whereabouts, Mica has a considerably easier time navigating the world. Slim in build with shoulder-length light brown hair and dressed in fashionable and chic clothing, male characters are drawn to her for her beauty and charm and are interested in helping her navigate Warsaw's streets and bureaucracy. Mica is personable and easily able to enter conversations with people wherever she goes, and she is at ease in both serious and lighthearted exchanges and cries when she is upset and emotional. Yet Mica is not a simplistic female character who exploits her sensitivity, beauty, and charm to manipulate others' emotions in order to secure favors. As a recently orphaned young adult, Mica eschews simple categorization, demonstrating a femininity that is both complex and oppositional to hegemonic Israeli femininity. As Modan makes clear in a scene early in the book when Mica defends her grandmother from a young man who makes fun of Regina, Mica has strong principles for which she is willing to stand up. In that particular scene, a young traveler mocks Regina for not wanting to dispose of her water bottle before passing through airport security; in response, Mica falsely tells the security agent that the young man is smuggling drugs in his luggage.[17] Later, when she learns that Tomasz hopes to turn Regina's biography into a graphic novel, Mica reacts with righteous indignation over perceived financial exploitation of Regina's experiences.[18] She temporarily breaks up with Tomasz and refuses to let him have his sketchbook back. Mica's intellectual and emotional awareness is buttressed by physical prowess. In one of the text's most humorous scenes, an accountant, who she hopes can help her, learns that she is Israeli and then brandishes a carrot, trying to attack her. Mica immediately disarms the man and returns his carrot; impressed with her counterattack, he subsequently reveals that he is trying to learn the Israeli martial art of Krav Maga. Mica explains to him that she actually is an expert in Krav Maga, having taught it to soldiers during her service in the Israeli army. She then proceeds to demonstrate the complicated move to the man so that he can perform it himself, before eventually moving on to discuss her family's lost property with him.[19] Mica's role in the army involved physicality, and yet her appearance and mannerisms do not reflect an adoption of hegemonic masculine traits like those of the women studied by Orna Sasson-Levy;[20]

instead, Mica managed to retain her sense of self and feminine identity even as she entered and assumed a leadership role within a traditionally masculine domain.

Mica's ability and willingness to go against societal expectations allows her to model an alternative form of femininity. This femininity is most clearly evident in how she mirrors Regina's earlier dating experiences with Roman by beginning her own sexual relationship with Tomasz. At one point early in the graphic novel, Mica and Tomasz's burgeoning relationship is criticized by Regina. Oblivious to the irony at play given her own past relationship with Roman, Regina worries that Tomasz might be an anti-Semite and that he could be dangerous, or that his grandparents might have even murdered Jews in the Holocaust. In relation to this scene, Kevin Haworth notes that, while it is true that Regina is acting as an overprotective grandmother, her comments belie "the suspicion with which Jews regard their non-Jewish European counterparts" in the pale of the Holocaust.[21] Regina's fears about Tomasz stand in marked contrast to Tamara's concerns with As'ad in *Farm 54*. Regina is not concerned about Tomasz's status solely as a non-Jew who might corrupt the Jewish-Israeli girl, nor do her concerns stem from a place wherein Israeli national identity and ethos are elevated over other groups. Instead, they are rooted in historical, as opposed to national, concerns. At the same time, however, Regina's explicit concerns do question Mica's agency and ability to freely make choices as an independent woman and, prior to going to Tomasz's home for a first date, Mica explains to Regina that she is not a child and is capable of making her own choices and, if need be, of defending herself.

By choosing to partner Mica with Tomasz alongside Regina's indifference to him not being Israeli, Modan depicts an alternative form of Israeli femininity which moves beyond preserving and promoting Israeliness as the defining feature of the Israeli woman. While Mica and Tomasz are not yet even in a committed relationship by the graphic novel's end, they do plan to remain in contact and meet up in the future. Their willingness to explore what that might look like, as a long-distance international and interfaith couple, testifies to an adoption of alternative Israeli femininity. Advocating for her femininity by way of sexual exploration with Tomasz recreates the past and returns the Ashkenazi Jewish woman to Europe and to the type of men women of her community had once been with, as opposed to the new Jewish man that populates Israel. This is a femininity which directly challenges the hegemonic Israeli ideal, and both Haworth and Assaf Gamzou note how Mica and Tomasz's relationship challenges Israeli expectations about dating because she is dating a European non-Jew.[22]

Exploring her femininity in this way also allows Mica to model a femininity that opposes the strict bifurcation that has shaped the ways that Israelis view themselves as different or other in relation to their Arab neighbors and much of the wider world. By embracing an alternative form of femininity, Mica shows how reconciliation with even the most historically antagonistic of peoples is possible. Tomasz and Mica's relationship effectively models what Froma Zeitlin calls the "process of reconstructing the past as filtered through the consciousness (and complicity) of a belated witness in the fusion of then and now".[23] Mica and Tomasz move beyond facile us-versus-them understandings of Polish–Jewish relationships to show that deep understanding, appreciation, and even reconciliation can be achieved. They banter and discuss love and loss and what each finds sexy. Through the new connections that materialize, an emotional and psychical homeostasis can be established, and a new – albeit different – Polish–Jewish relationship can emerge and, with that, an alternative Israeli femininity.

Modan's text offers a fictional graphic depiction of how Erica Lehrer understands developments in the Polish town of Kazimierz. There, Jews and Poles regularly interact in ways that extend beyond the Holocaust and the suffering of Jews by way of intentional and purposeful meetings framed around shared Polish–Jewish culture and history. Lehrer sees in Kazimierz a "unique arena in which Jewish and Polish collective memories and national identities can be confronted, questioned, and expanded … [in ways that involve] counter-hegemonic political and moral concerns".[24] Like the budding relationship between Mica and Tomasz, which questions strict differentiations between religion and nationality, Lehrer argues that the city's approach to commemoration "actively call[s] into question rigidly defined notions of Polishness and Jewishness".[25]

The worlds of Kazimierz and Modan's Warsaw are not fairy-tale settings with magical moments. They represent genuine attempts to find "conciliatory space that works against more conflictive notions of Poland's Jewish heritage that pit Jewishness and Polishness against one another".[26] As seen with Mica, who is forced to reckon with Tomasz's own understanding of the Holocaust and how it also harmed Poles, opportunities for genuine listening to each other's experiences can create new societies which are built not on a competition of more traumatic suffering, but instead around collective hearing and healing. Mica's willingness to engage with a femininity that is sensitive to non-Israelis is especially evident in one of the concluding scenes of the text. Mica meets Roman for the first time and tells him that she is happy that he has retained possession of the apartment after so many years.[27] Through this acknowledgement, Mica reaffirms his right to her family's historic land, and she recognizes that he, too, lost his family as a result of the war through Regina's need to emigrate from Poland with their unborn child. Mica's solidarity with the other is similar to Noga's when she witnesses the destruction of a family's home, and yet Mica's ability to directly engage with the suffering in the moment contrasts with Noga's, given Noga's inability to actualize her feelings of distress and discomfort. Doing so establishes a femininity that is at once recognizable as Israeli in its willingness to protect and preserve life and dignity but simultaneously alien in its ability to transcend specific geographic borders and nationalities, prioritizing humanity over ethnicity and nationality.

Envisioning a Western woman in Asaf Hanuka's "The Realist"

Unlike Asaf Hanuka's rich and robust depictions of the ways that he confronts hegemonic masculinity in Israeli society as he analyzes his own experiences in "The Realist",[28] his depictions of his wife are, in comparison, bland and staid, lacking depth and detail on her thoughts and ideas. Given the series' weekly print run of over a decade, this is not accidental. But neither should it be interpreted as disinterest in her life. Instead, Hanuka's autobiographical focus and interest lies in mining *his* lived experiences for material suitable for publication. As a result, weekly comics that feature Hilit – who is not mentioned by name even once in the entire series[29] – tend to be either depictions of her behavior in relation to Hanuka or Hanuka's interpretations of her behavior. Despite not having a window into Hilit's own understanding of her femininity, Hanuka's comics provide the reader with an opportunity to consider how *he* understands femininity in Israeli society based on how he depicts his wife. Considering Hanuka's work in this way allows for an assessment of the ways that an Israeli male interprets femininity and a consideration of whether his depictions reflect hegemonic femininity or whether, like the comics of Modan and the Seliktars, they challenge the hegemony by articulating alternative constructions of femininity.

Hanuka's comics that depict statements made or behaviors performed by his wife tend to present a woman who is most at home with Western notions of femininity, as she is comfortable enjoying traditional material aspects of Western culture like going shopping while also demanding equality in her relationship with him. In "Perfect Pair", Hanuka illustrates the couple in a shoe store, with Hilit trying on numerous pairs in order to find the right fit. Her happiness at finding the pair she wants to buy is palpable as she models the pair in the store. Asleep in the corner, Hanuka is oblivious to his wife's shopping experience and her excitement. Hilit's ability to find contentment in material objects and to enjoy the experience irrespective of Asaf is indicative of a femininity that neither revolves around the masculine figure in her life nor is dependent upon it. Instead, her comfort with being happy with herself is indicative of a femininity that is altogether foreign to the hegemonic ideal. Elsewhere, in "Round Twelve", Hanuka illustrates himself boxing with Hilit. The two exchange many punches and both are left bloody by the end of the fight. In the penultimate panel, the fight is over and the two are shown hugging each other while recovering from the toils of boxing. In the final panel, Hanuka illustrates the two of them lying in bed, unscathed and with scowls on their face, revealing that the boxing fight was a metaphor for an argument that has remained unresolved (Figure 2.2). By presenting Hilit as capable of fighting against him, Hanuka legitimizes her non-traditional femininity and recognizes her right to disagree and argue with him. This is an identification of a femininity that sees women being allowed to disagree with their husbands and to not be subservient to them.

In addition to illustrating his wife's interest (and his disinterest) in shoe shopping, Hanuka also shares with readers his wife's expectations of him and the ways that he fails to live up to these expectations. In a comic entitled "Listen to Your Heart", Hanuka is chastised by Hilit for wanting to spend time at work instead of spending time with his family shopping for a gift for a party his parents are hosting. Her contention that Hanuka is too preoccupied with work and not preoccupied enough with his family demonstrates an inversion of the expected hegemonic behavior. Hilit's concern that Hanuka is too invested in the office – the traditional masculine domain – and not concerned enough with the family demonstrates an expectation that Hanuka shift away from demonstrations of hegemonic masculinity while simultaneously suggesting that investing and taking part in family relationships is a non-gendered expectation and is obligatory for men too. Elsewhere, in a comic titled "Rest", when Hilit is bedbound while sick at home, she becomes sad that Hanuka failed to check in on her or even offer her a glass of water (despite feeding and taking care of the children). Comics like "Rest" and "Listen to Your Heart" raise fundamental questions about the ways that men should be expected to behave in relation to their spouse and family. Hanuka's willingness to share his wife's disappointment with his behavior in a public forum is an important acknowledgement that he has failed to live up to her expectations. In light of Hanuka's comics "Brave Heart", "Deadlines", and Burp Man", which were considered in the last chapter, it is clear that Hanuka loves his family very much and, as shown in "Deadlines", he spends his workday

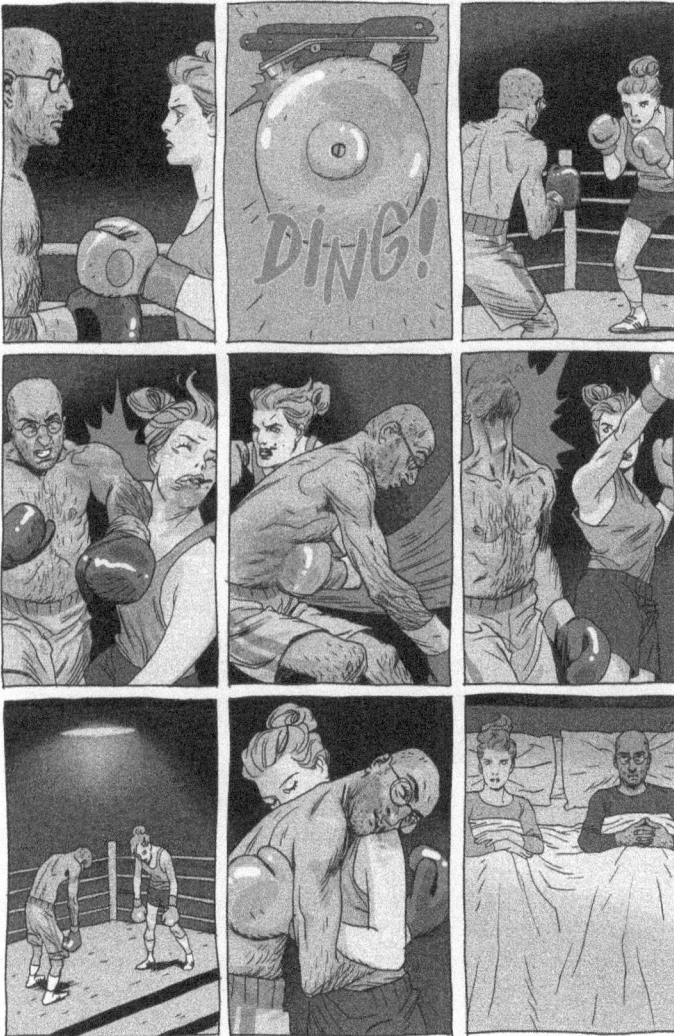

Figure 2.2 Asaf and Hilit Hanuka fighting and arguing. Credit: Asaf Hanuka, "Round 12," The Realist (Los Angeles: Archaia, 2015).

looking forward to being able to return home to play with his children. As well, while Hanuka is illustrated having fun while playing with his children in that comic, it is important to note that in the background Hilit is preparing dinner for the family. Furthermore, what is not shown in "Deadlines" is how much time he spends away from the family each day or what responsibilities Hilit has while he is at work. Hanuka's desire to be with his wife and children does little to mitigate the reality that he is not actually with them; and so when Hilit is confronted by his interest in working and not being with the family in "Listen to Your Heart" or not checking to see how she is feeling in "Rest", she becomes frustrated with his behavior. At the end of "Listen to Your Heart", it is telling that Hanuka has chosen to spend the afternoon with Hilit. His decision to go shopping with her to buy the gift intimates that Hanuka has not only acceded to Hilit's expectation of him but understood that this is what he should do as an equal partner in the marriage. By exposing Hilit's unconventional femininity, Hanuka legitimizes her expectations and recognizes that his gendered behavior must change in response to hers.

There are certain ways in which Hanuka's depiction of Hilit does reflect elements of hegemonic femininity. In "Rice Should be Eaten with a Spoon", Hilit desperately wants to prepare rice in the same way that Hanuka's Middle Eastern Iraqi mom does because she knows that he loves his mother's ethnic cuisine so much. As an Ashkenazi[30] woman who is not well versed in Iraqi cuisine, Hilit interviews Hanuka and his mother about the dish, frantically writing copious notes in order to prepare the rice to meet Hanuka's exacting standards. While Hilit's attention to Hanuka's food palate is certainly nice, wanting to cook the dish in this meticulously detailed way is also indicative of hegemonic femininity. By wanting to copy Hanuka's mother by being able to pre-pare food in this perfect way, Hilit hopes to assume the role of primary woman in his life, replacing his need to rely on his mother to meet his basic needs. But even in these instances of hegemonic femininity, Hilit subverts the historical model in subtle and creative ways. Hilit comes to realize that she will never prepare the rice dish in quite the same way as his mother; instead, she goes to a local Iraqi restaurant where the chefs prepare food like Hanuka's mother does and she purchases him rice. Upon returning home, Hanuka happily announces that Hilit has made the rice just like his mom does, and he says that she is the best. Hilit's creative solution involves a recognition that she is unable to do certain things in the way that Hanuka's mom does but that she is still able to assume a primary role in his life. Simultaneously subverting the gender norm while also reinforcing it is indicative of an attempt to make the hegemony work for her by adopting aspects of it which suit her needs – removing Hanuka's dependence on his mother and establishing her primacy – while replacing or modifying others that she cannot perform – preparing rice like a Middle Eastern Mizrahi.

Wanting to prepare food for Hanuka is not the only way that Hilit adopts elements of femininity while simultaneously challenging them. "The Man Who Wasn't There" is a four-panel comic that spans approximately a decade in their relationship, as evidenced by Hanuka's receding hairline and the evolution of their apartment's décor. In this beautifully illustrated comic, Hanuka positions himself lying down, being asked relationship questions by Hilit. In each of the first three panels, she asks one question; she asks whether Hanuka loves her, whether he wants to get married, and whether he wants to have children. In reply to each question, Hanuka says "yea, sure". Hilit's willingness to ask these relationship questions is emblematic of the hegemonic feminine ideal where women assume responsibility for the family domain. Here, taken to its extreme, Hilit seeks control and clarity within the relationship while Hanuka remains passively indifferent to her. As the individual in charge of the family's decisions, Hilit establishes the parameters of their relationship, determining their statuses as a couple and as parents. In the strip's culminating panel, Hilit makes one final decision for the family and she announces that she is divorcing Hanuka. Fed up with Hanuka's unwillingness to assume greater responsibility within the family dynamic, she subverts her assigned gendered role as manager of the home by dissolving the partnership. In real life, Hanuka and Hilit remain married and so the final panel is fictional, but it is indicative of the ways that Israeli women who are unwilling to subscribe to gendered expectations are able to make use of these expectations in ways that benefit and suit their needs in the twenty-first century. Like "Rest" and "Listen to Your Heart", it is also a call to men to re-evaluate their own understandings of the ways that gender is constructed in Israeli society and to consider what role they are playing in maintaining hegemony or challenging it.

Hanuka's own understanding of the nature of his wife's femininity and the ways that she challenges hegemonic depictions is made most clear in the comics where he not only includes depictions of things that she says and does but weaves in his own commentary on them. In her analysis of Jewish American women's comics, Tahneer Oksman has suggested that there is a strong tendency to eschew the fantastical in favor of the literal. She contends that this has been done in order to avoid associations with superhero comics.[31] Similarly, the Israeli comics tradition also tends to avoid elements of the fantastical, prioritizing narratives set in the present. As a genre trying to establish its legitimacy and seriousness, this tendency by Israeli artists may reflect a similar fear of being associated with the superhero genre. Additionally, I contend that as part of an attempt to critique elements of Israeli society, retaining an emphasis on depicting its current manifestations facilitates a greater opportunity for deconstruction than by situating the comics in alternative Israels. Asaf Hanuka's work often diverges from the general trend to avoid the fantastical, as the most frequent narrative device employed by Hanuka is the inclusion of science fiction or fantasy elements into the comic strips. Hanuka uses fantastical elements in order to make sense of the real world that surrounds him.

The concept of fantastical autography helps make meaning of the comics where he employs otherworldly elements. Gillian Whitlock and Anna Poletti have coined the term *autography* to refer specifically to texts that are visual autobiographies. They define the term as "life narrative fabricated in and through drawing and design using various technologies, modes, and materials. A practice of reading the signs, symbols and techniques of visual arts in life narratives".[32] Through the creation of autography, the author chooses to "negotiate in and through"[33] visual media to tell his or her narrative. The autography is therefore a fusion between the genres of visual arts and autobiography. What distinguishes traditional fantasy literature from fantastical autography is that whereas the former is wholly fictional, the latter involves the conjoining of both fantastical and autobiographical – fictional and nonfictional – into a cohesive unit in which the real and imagined worlds blend together to create something wholly new. In Hanuka's case, the use of fantasy provides the reader with a new way of understanding Israeli society by presenting an estrangement of the familiar. While still heavily grounded in nonfictional and autobiographical experiences, the fantastical allows the reader to recognize that hidden below the surface is a world that is rich with meaning and symbolism, and a world that is at once similar to and different from the real world. What emerges most clearly from Hanuka's work is that his use of the fantastical in his autography enables him to make use of complex visual metaphors to offer commentary on Israeli society and his place in it. More often than not, Hanuka's presentation of the "real" world is that it is bleak and dreary, but fantasy provides him with a way of interpreting and recasting this world in new and alternate ways. These ways allow him to escape – even if momentarily – from the real world and, through the fantastic, be able to see it differently.

Hanuka has produced three comics where he integrates fantastical elements in relation to his depiction of Hilit. All three of the comics reflect, in some way, Hanuka's own insecurities and fears that he is undeserving of Hilit, that he must become a better man, and that, if he does not, he becomes replaceable by someone or something better than him. Whereas previously discussed comics like "The Man Who Wasn't There" depict their relationship in the real world without providing much insight into how he would feel about Hilit leaving, the integration of fantastical elements introduces Hanuka's anxieties with regards to his wife. In a comic written for the Jewish holiday of Purim,[34] Hanuka illustrates his family dressed as comic book characters; accompanying each illustration is a brief statement of the family member's core values which justifies their chosen superhero. Hilit is dressed as Catwoman and Hanuka writes about her: "mom: her beauty is a disguise. Her secret weapon is her brain, but her source of power is her heart. And it isn't wrapped in a bow. It's real".[35] Catwoman is a misunderstood character in DC Comics' Batman series. Initially presented as a villain who steals jewels, she has invariably been understood as an anti-hero, someone who does good but not always in the most ethical way. The use of the fantastical superhero provides insight into how Hanuka understands the ways that Hilit sometimes behaves. While he might not always like what his wife does or says, she always does it for the right reasons and in order to do what is best for the family. Reading "Only Once a Year" through the prism of "Listen to Your Heart" renders Hanuka's ultimate decision to accept Hilit's chastisement about the ways that he prioritizes his family even more understandable. Hanuka shows that he understands the importance of Hilit and her expression of a femininity because it is a femininity that challenges him to be a better man by behaving like less of a hegemonic Israeli male. Like Catwoman, who at times makes the characters around her uncomfortable despite her good intentions, Hanuka has come to recognize Hilit's role and expression of femininity within the family unit as essential to its success.

In two comics Hanuka transforms Hilit into a supernatural monster that causes him physical or emotional harm. In "That Day of the Month", Hilit quickly becomes angry with Hanuka while he is checking his email in bed. She reveals a laundry-list of grievances to a stupefied Hanuka before turning into a werewolf and eating his body, with only his skull left remaining on the bed. In "Upgrade", an Apple-product-loving vampire bites Hilit, rendering her addicted to Apple products and demanding an iPhone. After acquiring her new phone, she comes to love it so much that she realizes that Hanuka is now superfluous to her despite his protests to the contrary and she announces that she is permanently leaving him for her iPhone. The fantastical elements of werewolves and vampires provide insight into the ways that Hanuka attempts to understand moments when her behavior is irrational or unexplainable.

Visualizing Hilit's menstruation cycle and the concomitant conflicts that result as a feral beast belies his own uncertainty with how to behave or act around her so that she does not chew his head off. Similarly, turning Hilit into a tech-junkie who, after getting her fix, realizes that nothing else in her life – including her family that she loves so much – matters or has meaning indicates confusion at her newfound obsession. What both comics show is insecurity. Having already established that he does not feel worthy of her, the use of fantastical beasts offers Hanuka an opportunity to share his fear that Hilit will leave him. It is noteworthy that once Hanuka realizes that something is different with Hilit, he becomes far more attentive to her words and mannerisms, modifying his behavior in relation to hers. He professes his love for her, expecting her to respond in kind, but she does not; instead, she consumes him or abandons him. These moments of confusion suggest that, for Hanuka, a barrier remains between the masculine and feminine where he still does not fully understand his wife, but Hanuka's willingness to adapt his staid masculinity into an attentive relationship-oriented masculinity testifies to his desire to earn Hilit's respect and favor as an equal partner in their relationship.

It is crucial to call attention to the reality that both masculinity and femininity operate in relation to the other. In the previous chapter, I argued that rejecting hegemonic masculinity involves creating a space that recognizes the feminine other and which elevates certain personality traits over others. Here, on the other hand, rejecting traditional notions of femininity involves abandoning behaviors and attitudes that have been forced upon women with regards to how men expect them to behave. *The Property*, "The Realist", and *Farm 54* all introduce complex characters who express their femininity in ways that run counter to the historical ideal and who adopt aspects of the hegemony while rejecting others. This process is different for each of the characters depending on what best suits their individual needs and suggests that, while the hegemonic model might no longer be relevant in contemporary Israeli society, no single model for femininity has replaced it. Instead, more liberal and fluid models are present, coexisting together, furthering more varied and nuanced understandings of femininity in Israeli society.

What unites the female characters is the notion that they are not dependent on motherhood as the cornerstone of their identities, and nor are their roles as mothers (or future mothers) the primary way that they define themselves. Instead, the authors and illustrators depict women doing everyday activities – things which are normal elsewhere in the world – but in the heavily gendered landscape of Israel, these activities take on added meaning and weight. Depictions of women kissing intimately, forming friendships with Arabs, dating non-Jews and demanding emotional availability from their partners all challenge the mythology of the stoic woman who serves her country by birthing the future soldiers and mothers of Israel. What Hanuka, the Seliktars, and Modan offer the reader is an insight into an Israeli femininity that espouses alternative gender norms and that allows women to construct their own identities as members of an Israeli society not defined by narratives of war and death. This femininity does not place men at the core of a woman's identity or sacrifice as its primary value; instead, it locates femininity – in its myriad meanings and complexities – as the core of a woman's identity and her own values as most primary. This is a femininity which has come to reject the stakes made upon the bodies and souls of Israeli women and in its stead offers up multiple alternative ways for expressing femininity within Israeli society.

Notes

1 Seliktar and Seliktar, *Farm 54*.
2 Seliktar and Seliktar, *Farm 54*.
3 Harris, *Warriors, Witches, Whores*, 150.
4 Harris, *Warriors, Witches, Whores*, 183.
5 Harris, *Warriors, Witches, Whores*, 179.
6 Lambert, "Sex, Violence".
7 Seliktar and Seliktar, *Farm 54*.
8 Seliktar and Seliktar, *Farm 54*.
9 Seliktar and Seliktar, *Farm 54*.
10 Hauser, "We Rule the Base", 645.
11 Seliktar and Seliktar, *Farm 54*.
12 Seliktar and Seliktar, *Farm 54*.
13 Michel, "Panels for Peace", 222.
14 Jacobson, "Intimate Relations", 35.
15 Biographical details of Modan are included in Chapter 1 in the section on *Exit Wounds*.
16 Ronen, "Post-Holocaust Representations", 20.
17 Modan, *The Property*, 5–9.
18 Modan, *The Property*, 147–149.
19 Modan, *The Property*, 59–66.
20 Sasson-Levy, "Constructing Identities".
21 Haworth, *The Comics of Rutu Modan*, 128.
22 Haworth, *The Comics of Rutu Modan*, 128, and Gamzou, "Third-Generation Graphic Syndrome", 233–234.
23 Zeitlin, "The Vicarious Witness", 7.
24 Lehrer, "Can there Be?", 272.
25 Lehrer, "Can there Be?", 282.

26 Lehrer, "Can there Be?", 272.

27 Modan, *The Property*, 219.

28 Readers can find introductory remarks about Asaf Hanuka and his comic series "The Realist" in Chapter 1, where his approach to hegemonic masculinity is addressed in detail.

29 Hilit's name is listed on Hanuka's personal website in his biography; this can be found at www.asafhanuka.com/about-1.

30 Blonde-haired and blue-eyed, Hilit's complexion is pale, especially in contrast to Hanuka's much darker Middle Eastern Mizrahi – Judeo-Arab – complexion. While not directly mentioned in the series, there are many allusions to Hilit descending from a family of Askenazi – Eastern European – Jews and to the fact that, because of their different ethnicities, Hanuka considers himself part of a mixed marriage. Historically, Ashkenazi Israelis frowned upon marriages with Mizrahim, but today, these marriages are far more common and accepted.

31 Oksman, *How Come Boys*, 18.

32 Whitlock and Poletti, "Self-Regarding Art", v.

33 Whitlock, "Autographics", 969.

34 Purim is a Jewish holiday that celebrates the nullification by the Persian king Ahasuerus of a genocidal decree against the Jewish people. It is customary to dress up in costume on the day of the festival and to attend parties and parades which celebrate the Jewish people's salvation.

35 Hanuka, *The Realist: Plug and Play*.

3 Gender, minorities, and the Hebrew graphic novel

Matt Reingold

The preceding two chapters can be characterized by presence – the presence of a community of Israeli writers and artists producing graphic novels about Israel, the presence of a corpus of texts that introduce complex characters and themes from a small country, the presence of a distinct identity in the Israeli graphic novel genre, the presence of an English-language publishing industry interested in Israeli graphic novelists. While not defined by gender, challenging normative gender constructs is a central feature of the Israeli graphic novel, and in this sense, the genre is both transgressive and progressive. In this chapter, I move away from the English-language Israeli graphic novel and consider graphic novels that have been primarily published for the Israeli reader. I do so out of a recognition of the limitations of the graphic novels that have been analyzed thus far and the more expansive opportunities available for understanding Israeli society by considering texts constructed for local readers.

With regards to gender, I have hopefully made a convincing argument about the expansiveness of the Israeli graphic novel oeuvre and the ways that English-language Israeli graphic novels challenge normative gender constructs. The progressiveness that is readily apparent with regards to gender obfuscates a noticeable omission in the translated texts. Despite introducing liberal notions of gender, among the Israeli graphic novels that have been published in English there are noticeable ways that hegemonic aspects of Israeli society are reinforced through the exclusion of primary characters from minority communities.[1] In particular, English-language Israeli graphic novels have not yet been released which prominently feature any Palestinian-Arab citizens of Israel, Orthodox/traditional Jewish Israelis, Ethiopian-Israelis, or LGBTQ Israelis as main characters. These communities constitute close to 50 per cent of the Israeli population. Moving beyond protagonists,

DOI: 10.4324/9781003150435-4

the lone text that even features a minority character in a meaningful role is the Seliktars' *Farm 54*, and As'ad is only on page for the first part of the story. None of the other graphic novels feature any of these minority communities. A running joke in Hanuka's "The Realist" is that he is sometimes mistaken for being an Orthodox Jew because he doesn't always shave his beard or an Arab because of his dark complexion, yet Arabs are never depicted, and Orthodox Jews only serve as bit characters when illustrated in the background of panels. Even Rutu Modan's *Exit Wounds*, a text that is set during the height of the Second Palestinian Intifada, does not include a single Arab character.

In this chapter, I will show that these characters do exist, albeit in graphic novels primarily marketed for Israeli readers. While most of these texts are far more niche with regards to the audiences that they speak to, they also introduce alternative conceptions of gender that have not been previously considered in this book, which I will explore here. I will accomplish these two goals by exploring minority representation in Michel Kichka's *Second Generation: The Things I Didn't Tell My Father* and *Falafel with Hot Sauce*, lesbian author Ilana Zeffren's short stories "Zina" and "Holidays", and religious nationalist Shay Charka's *Beyond the Line*.

Navigating the past and the present in Michel Kichka's *Second Generation: Things I Didn't Tell My Father* and *Falafel with Hot Sauce*

Belgian-Israeli Michel Kichka immigrated to Israel in 1974 when he was 20 years old. Kichka was raised in a secular-Zionist home in Liège, Belgium. Both of his parents were Holocaust survivors, but whereas his mother's entire family was saved, Kichka's father lost most of his relatives. Kichka has published two autobiographical graphic novels about his experiences growing up in Belgium and his life in Israel. Both were first published in French, Kichka's native language, before being translated into Hebrew. Kichka's work is available for English speakers as digital texts on online platforms like Amazon's Kindle store and ComiXology, a popular comics app. Despite ease of access, however, Kichka's work is not particularly well-known among English readers, and it is for this reason that I have included them in this chapter. His first graphic novel, *Second Generation: Things I Didn't Tell My Father*, was published in 2016 by Europe Comics and is primarily about Kichka's experiences as a second-generation Holocaust survivor and the ways that his father's time spent in Nazi concentration camps would shape the way that he parented and raised Michel and his three siblings. The second graphic novel, *Falafel with Hot Sauce*, also published by Europe Comics, was released in 2019 and is about Kichka's time spent in Israel, including the summers he volunteered in the country before he decided to immigrate.

The two graphic novels complement each other because, even though they focus on different topics, they have considerable chronological overlap and sketch a complex portrait of a bifurcated life spent in both Europe and Israel. At the same time that Kichka explores living in the shadow of the Holocaust in *Second Generation*, he celebrates his sexual freedom in Israel in *Falafel with Hot Sauce*. In *Second Generation*, Kichka demonstrates so many of the masculine traits that were rejected by Israelis, while in *Falafel with Hot Sauce*, his masculinity has shifted, embodying elements of hegemonic Zionist Israeli masculinity. Considered together, Kichka's works reify the complexities of gender, refusing to accept or prefer one version over the other; instead, competing and complimentary masculinities work in concert with each other, producing an altogether new approach towards Israeli masculinity for the twenty-first century.

Stylistically, Kichka's two graphic novels employ a consistent cartoony line, with exaggerated facial features and bodies. Where the two works differ, however, is with regards to color. Whereas *Second Generation* is illustrated with a black and white palette, *Falafel with Hot Sauce* is illustrated with a rich and vibrant color palette. Illustrating the Holocaust and European Jewish life in black and white and Israel in color is reflective of a worldview that sees Europe as listless and inhospitable for Jews, and Israel as a site for the continuation of the Jewish cultural experience. Kichka's decision to simultaneously depict himself as moribund in Europe and alive in Israel is reflective of traditional Israeli narratives which position Israel as the solution to anti-Semitism. Examples of purported weak masculinity abound in *Second Generation*. Kichka experiences nightmares as a child while also craving love and relationship with his father. Lola Serraf locates in Kichka's entire existence a link to the past, given that he is named after a deceased ancestor and that all of Michel's successes are really a way for his father "to show his persecutors that they have failed to ruin him".[2] Furthermore, following the tragic suicide of his younger brother Charly – acknowledged only in *Second Generation* despite chronologically taking place after his immigration to Israel – Kichka illustrates himself performing masculine behaviors that are negatively associated with pre-state Jews. He is moribund, consumed with death, crying uncontrollably, depressed, perseverating over why Charly has taken his own life (Figure 3.1). Illustrating himself in this way is a recognition of his suffering, but this is a suffering

Figure 3.1 Michel Kichka saddened by his brother's suicide. Credit: Michel Kichka, *Second Generation: The Things I Didn't Tell My Father*, translated by Montana Kane, (Paris: Europe Comics, 2016), 60.

that is connotative of a masculinity that is foreign to Israel because of the emotional vulnerability that Kichka expresses. Conversely, in *Falafel with Hot Sauce*, Kichka and his wife Olivia adopt many aspects of hegemonic Israeli gender norms. Despite his disinterest, he enlists in the army and tries to live up to his female commander's hegemonic mantra: "I have three weeks to make you into men".[3] Later, he illustrates cheerful family photos of each of his three sons as they are conscripted into the army, and he plays the role of proud and supportive father while Olivia assumes her maternal role as for "twelve years … Olivia washed, dried, folded, and put away their khaki uniform".[4]

While Michel and Olivia do adopt aspects of the hegemony, there are many ways that they simultaneously challenge the Jewish-Israeli hegemony while not reverting to the European model of Jewry that had been rejected by early Zionists. Kichka illustrates a number of scenes where both he and his wife refuse to be bullied into positions that make them uncomfortable. Upon learning that his sister's husband has been called up to the Israeli army, Kichka flies to Israel from Belgium in order to help her take care of her child. Assuming the role of co-parent alongside her, Kichka models the imperative that gendered parenting roles are circumspect and that whoever is able to help should do so irrespective of gender. Describing his initial decision to fly to Israel, Kichka writes: "If I can't help the country, at least I can help my sister".[5] What Kichka only comes to realize when he is a parent himself is that it is by taking care of children and raising them that he is also able to help the country. Elsewhere, Olivia embodies Israeli femininity by growing plants in her front yard and by laundering her children's military uniforms; she also comes to reject the hegemony by audibly protesting in the streets, demanding change in institutions that she sees as corrupt. Kichka compares the protests that Olivia and her fellow demonstrators stage to an open Caesarian-section wound that is birthing a new stage in the evolution of Israeli society. Illustrating Israel using maternal and feminine imagery connotes a departure from the dominant masculinity that has shaped Israeli society since its founding. Kichka's illustration of the map of Israel bleeding at its mid-point in the Dead Sea powerfully evokes the tension that he palpably feels and that is taking over Israeli society, and the resistance that is emerging over the conflict between different Israelis (Figure 3.2). The wound remains open, unhealing, as protests and counterprotests over the nature and shape of the Israel of the future emerge, exposing craters in the country's foundation.

Figure 3.2 Israel bleeding following a caesarean birth. Credit: Michel Kichka, *Falafel with Hot Sauce*, translated by Montana Kane (Paris: Europe Comics, 2019), 54.

What Kichka envisions for this new Israel is made very clear in *Falafel with Hot Sauce*. He openly and warmly recognizes relationships with Arab-Palestinian citizens of Israel. He proudly illustrates his son David refusing to dehumanize a Palestinian prisoner by making him run after the military vehicle because there was no space inside it for him. He warmly reflects on the relationships he has built with Arabs who live both inside and outside Israel and who participate in cartooning workshops with him. In a scene where his son Elie is lying in a hospital bed with a mysterious illness, Kichka acknowledges the intelligence and medical expertise of the Arab physician who is able to cure Elie based on his understanding of the Arab villages where Elie served while in the army. Furthermore, Kichka models humility, recognizing that the Jewish-Israeli doctors were unable to save Elie and it was *only* an Arab doctor who was able to successfully intervene and save Elie's life. Kichka's exploration of the Arab-Palestinian sector of Israel introduces perspectives that have been absent in the Israeli graphic novels that have been considered thus far. His willingness not only to critique his own society but to positively feature and promote inclusion and understanding models the type of Israeli society that he hopes will exist. This is an Israeli society that is at odds with the hegemonic Israel but is one that is consistent with Kichka's own understanding of the world and the type of people Israeli society should produce. It is a society that recognizes the traumas of war, as evidenced by the impact of the Holocaust on his family, but one that refuses to allow Israelis to be beholden to a masculinity that is no longer relevant. For Kichka, Europe is not only depicted in black and white because of the Holocaust but also because of the weight of negative familial history and burdens. Instead, it is only in Israel where he can be independent of this weight and that he is able to live his life to the fullest. In Israel Kichka is capable of expressing himself in technicolor in a society that is built on foundations that have learned from the past, been shaped by the past, but are not repetitions of it. Kichka's texts testify to a worry that hegemonic masculinity and femininity produce an inversion of the historical Jewish experience in which Jews, by becoming strong and powerful, become the aggressors. Kichka does not negate the violence committed by Palestinian Arabs against Jewish Israelis; his pride in his son David's decision to refuse to allow Jewish-Israeli soldiers to mistreat a Palestinian man is a recognition that moral behavior is expected, even when others do not behave morally. It is also a recognition of the type of parenting that he has embraced; he will not be like his father, the man who ruined Kichka's and his siblings' childhoods. Instead, he will model a loyalty to values and, through this, allow his children to assume their own identities and not be limited by their parents' negative histories and experiences. Kichka's motivation to be a different father to his children than his father was to him reflects an evolution in the role of Israeli men as fathers based on his own experiences. Kichka recognizes that it is only by showing his children emotional vulnerability that he is able to model for them kindness and compassion, thereby allowing them to transcend their own familial and national histories, emerging as new twenty-first century Israeli men.

Religious awakenings in Shay Charka's *Beyond the Line*

Towards the end of *Falafel with Hot Sauce*, Kichka is asked by one of his college students why the majority of Israeli political cartoons emerge from the left side of the political spectrum. Kichka explains: "political cartoons are a form of opposition. Every artist wants to upset the established order that those in power want to maintain".[6] With the exception of a four-year period between November 2005 and March 2009, every government that has led Israel since 2001 has been a right-wing government helmed by either Ariel Sharon or Benjamin Netanyahu. If Kichka's contention about cartooning is correct, this can explain the absence of right-wing political cartoons, given an almost two-decade relationship between the established political order and the right-wing community.

A notable exception to this claim can be found in the pioneering autobiographical work of Shay Charka in his Hebrew-language series *Beyond the Line*. Charka's comics from *Beyond the Line* have been collected in two volumes that were published by Modan Press in 2008 and 2012, but they are only available for purchase in Israel.[7] A resident of Zufim, Charka is a religious nationalist[8] cartoonist whose comics are set in the West Bank settlement where he lives. His comics are regularly published in Makor Rishon, a right-wing religious nationalist newspaper. In many respects, Charka's comics depict exactly what would be expected from a member of a traditional religious right-wing settler community in Israel. Charka and his wife wear the typical uniform of the religious-nationalist community; he wears a knitted head covering and his wife wears a dress and a hat to cover her hair. Charka does not recognize the right of the Palestinian people to a state of their own called Palestine in parts of the West Bank or even Palestinian national identity.[9] In one comic, he reinforces hegemonic gender identities by illustrating himself expecting his wife to do the laundry for the family.[10] Elsewhere, he is dismissive of Reform Judaism, comparing its Jewish innovations to modernist pop art, as opposed to Orthodox Judaism, which has a more hallowed and revered tradition, like the great Impressionist masters.[11] As a settler, Charka also openly acknowledges feeling abandoned and betrayed by the Israeli government following its 2005 decision to dismantle Jewish communities in the Gaza Strip and to cede control of it to the Palestinian people. Whereas he once felt connected to the government and to secular Jewish Israelis, he shares that he found himself unable to visit the secular enclave of Tel Aviv in the months following the Disengagement from Gaza, and that upon his return to the city, he felt like a tourist visiting a foreign city, and not like a citizen returning home.[12]

Yet throughout the series, Charka subverts expectations of religious-nationalist Jews. Criticism of religious nationalists and Orthodox Jews is a fairly common trope in Israeli society and the media, with concerns relating to how their over-enlistment in the IDF has turned the once-secular military institution religious,[13] their general unwillingness to cede territory in the West Bank for the creation of a state for Palestinians,[14] and a religious ideology that is at odds with secular Jewish-Israeli society.[15] While Charka does not dispute the contention that his fellow settlers are outsiders within Israeli society, his comics reframe their experiences by presenting settlers as misunderstood victims of a normative Israeli society bent on rejecting any minority unwilling to join their homogenous culture. Charka inverts the narrative espoused by the mainstream by depicting alternative expressions of Israeliness; these depictions are actually similar to those of many of the other characters and authors that have been explored in this book.

Visually, one of the most unique features of Charka's comic strips is the pronounced nose that he draws on his own face. Indicative of anti-Semitism in historical illustrations, Charka's appropriation of the offensive trope serves as a commentary on Israeli society and the experiences of his religious community. Firstly, in light of Scott McCloud's understanding of how cartoonists illustrate faces,[16] Charka's depictions of an exaggerated cartoon nose necessitate that Israeli Jews recognize elements of sympathy with Charka as a fellow Jewish Israeli by dint of the use of a historical caricature that all Israelis would understand. Simultaneously, however, the nose also distances Charka from the rest of Israeli society. Other Jewish Israelis are not depicted with a large nose; the nose becomes a link between Charka and historical Jewish communities that have experienced persecution for being different. Here, the visual signifier of the nose connotes Charka's religious identity as a religious-nationalist Israeli who has experienced ostracization from normative Israeli society. The nose thus comes to both include Charka in the wider Jewish-Israeli experience while also distancing him

from Jewish Israelis who have been able to assimilate into the hegemonic majority.

One of the unique features of Charka's *Beyond the Line* is that he
genuinely purports to create a funny comic. While not every comic is
humorous, many of the comics end on a funny note or a surprise twist.
Charka's inclusion of humor disrupts hegemonic notions of religious
settlers and introduces nuances into how the community operates. In
"Favourite Son", Kichka and his rabbi wonder where Natan, a fellow
settler, has disappeared to; eventually they learn that Natan has travelled to Ukraine on a religious pilgrimage. In the penultimate panel,
the two wonder who is tending to Natan's goat while he is abroad. In
the final panel, Natan is shown on the airplane with his goat Ephraim
sitting beside him wearing a seatbelt.[17] In "Creative World", Charka
has been tasked with building a golem, a mythological monster that
protects Jewish communities. According to legend, written across the
golem's forehead is the Hebrew word *emet*, truth. Charka and the rabbi
debate the appropriateness of a right-wing settler writing the word *emet*
because the word is also the three-letter ballot box abbreviation[18] of
Israel's left-wing Labor party, a party that settlers vehemently oppose
given Labor's preference to dismantle West Bank settlements.[19] The
effect of comics like these on the reader is that they introduce a side to
religious nationalists that is not typically depicted in Israeli print media.
Presenting himself as both quirky and irreverent while also being a
settler blurs the lines between associations with the religious community and humanizes them by showing behaviors and mannerisms akin
to those of other non-religious Israelis. While the content of the jokes
might differ, given the differences between religious and secular communities and between left- and right-wing communities, humor transcends
all sectors of a society and is able to offer a non-hegemonic depiction of
a community that is often criticized.

A further way that Charka challenges assumptions about the religious nationalist settler community is by castigating members of secular
Israeli society over the assumptions that they make about settlers. In
"On the Line", a comic where a secular Israeli lectures Charka about
how "you people" care more about the sanctity of land than the sanctity of people, Charka uses the man's words against him, turning them
into a pun. The man's intention is to suggest that settlers prioritize
settling the West Bank irrespective of popular public opinion; Charka
chooses to interpret the man's "you people" as a reference to artists,
and he explains that he always pays attention to how he illustrates
both people and settings.[20] In "Prejudices", a taxi driver explains to
Charka that he is uncomfortable driving through Arab villages and

that he hates Arabs as much as Charka does. After Charka questions the cabdriver's assertion that settlers hate Arabs, he is told: "oh come on, it's well known! Settlers, sorry to be telling you this, don't take it hard, but they're racists with all sorts of prejudices".[21] The comic ends with Charka wondering what is known about cabdrivers. Considered together, the two comics offer a fascinating insight into understanding Charka's experiences in his settler community. Both of Charka's responses – clever wordplay and sarcastic rejoinders – do not involve actual responses to the contentions that either man makes. What is achieved, however, is a recognition of a double standard that is at play and which plagues the ways that his community is understood. Whether or not there are settlers who hate Arabs or there are settlers who care more about the land of Israel than the people of Israel is irrelevant; what matters is that there are secular Israelis who also have these viewpoints, but their voices have not permeated Israeli society. By depicting Israelis who claim to understand the settler community better than it understands itself, Charka calls attention to both the negative attention his community has received and the ways that it has come to define public perception, even if the views concerned are also espoused by members of the hegemony.

The most significant way that Charka distances himself from hegemonic Israeli society is through the formation of an allyship with Palestinian Arabs who live in the West Bank. Charka positions both the religious settlers *and* the Palestinian Arabs as opponents of the Israeli military and as victims of its aggression. Charka illustrates his Palestinian friend Ahmed warmly wishing him a happy Independence Day (and Charka wishing Ahmed a happy Nakba Day in return)[22] and his encounters with Israeli border security guards who use physical aggression against Jewish settlers,[23] and he even depicts himself as a victim of violence after being hit in the face by a police officer.[24] In "Aftershock", one of the series' most challenging comics, Charka sits with Ahmed following his violent confrontation with the Israeli army. Ahmed struggles to find the words to explain how Charka must be feeling; he eventually says that the police treated Charka just like they treat the Arabs (Figure 3.3). Charka builds suspense throughout the panel, focusing the reader's gaze on the left side of his face; only after Ahmed creates the parallel between Charka and Arabs is the reader shown the blackened eye on the right side of Charka's face. Charka's artistic choice to obfuscate his face until the very end allows for the reader to imaginatively construct their own narrative of what has happened to him and what has led to his new appreciation of Ahmed's experiences. Reserving the depiction of violence for the final panel contextualizes

Ahmed's comment and justifies Charka's decision to not respond to Ahmed as he has come to understand Ahmed's own experiences with Israeli police in a new light. At the same time, as an unexpected experience, Charka's silence also reflects Hillary Chute's claim that illustrating trauma "carries its own inchoate parallel, its own inarticulate shadow".[25] Reserving himself to only four words – and these words merely confirm the presence of additional security personnel at the site of violence – Charka's blackened eye serves as the main form of communication that he is capable of at this time, as he has been rendered mute by the trauma. With time, he might be able to articulate additional words, but in this comic, the illustration of violence serves as his traumatic testimonial.

Charka's illustration of violence, as symbolized through the black eye that mars his face, evokes feelings of disequilibrium for readers who tend to assume alliances between settlers and the Israeli military. Highlighting the mark upon his face and violence in general evokes comparisons to Chute's analysis of the impact of depictions of violence in non-fiction graphic novels and the images' power to testify as witnesses against the use of force. Chute writes that graphic narratives offer "an absorptive intimacy with their narratives while defamiliarizing received images of history".[26] Charka's willingness to testify to his own trauma at the hands of Jewish-Israeli soldiers serves as a visual signifier of his humiliation and debasement while simultaneously challenging accepted narratives of the triadic relationship between settlers, soldiers, and Palestinians which situate Palestinians acting in opposition to the other two.

Charka's illustrations present Israeli institutions as the obstacles to peace and as instigators of conflict between settlers and Palestinian Arabs. The irony that is not lost on readers is the highly complicated and contentious relationship that exists between settlers and West Bank Palestinians and the role that government bodies must play in order to mitigate conflict between the two groups. However, by highlighting the similarity between Palestinians and settlers, Charka creates an interesting equivocation between the two groups and a challenge to Israelis who sympathize with the plight of Palestinians but not with the settlers. What is also made abundantly clear throughout the series, and especially in "Aftershock", is the genuine relationship that exists between Ahmed and Charka. Contrary to an expectation that Palestinians and settlers operate antagonistically with each other, Charka depicts moments of levity, kindness, and compassion between two friends who have found common ground and formed a connection together amidst the conflict.

Figure 3.3 Ahmed sympathizing with Charka about being mistreated by
Israeli officers. Credit: Shay Charka, "Aftershock", January 26,
2010, http://shaycharka.blogspot.com/2010/01/2-18.html.

Despite the friendship that Charka illustrates between himself and
Ahmed, it must be acknowledged that, as a right-wing settler, there are
limits to Charka's relationship with Palestinians. Charka treads a fine
line between friendship with individual Palestinians and a rejection
of Palestinian nationality. In "Superhero", he refuses to recognize the
claim that the Palestinian people have a distinct nationality that merits
the establishment of a state.[27] While perhaps odious to many Israelis,
as the only settler political cartoonist with a significant footprint in
the Israeli media,[28] Charka's willingness to publicly share a highly
unpopular opinion within Israeli society with his readership is further
evidence of how *Beyond the Line* challenges hegemonic Israeli society.
Publicizing an opinion that no right-wing Prime Minister has publicly
suggested since the 1990s introduces a voice that locates a space on the
Israeli cartooning map for the right-wing reader.

Gender is also a focus in *Beyond the Line*, as Charka interrogates the
ways that women are marginalized within his Orthodox community. In
particular, Charka rejects the traditional notion that rabbinic authorities
can use religious power to inhibit women's independence and autonomy.

In "Women's Reading", a comic about the festival of Purim, Charka bristles when the community's rabbi acknowledges that according to Jewish law women are permitted to publicly read the sacred literature on the holiday but says that he will not permit women to do so because increasing women's roles within the community can be a slippery slope that must be guarded against so that women's roles are not expanded by too much. The rabbi promulgates a religious Jewish stance known as fence-building; in order to prevent the community from breaking rules about what is and what is not permissible for women to do, a metaphoric fence is built around the actual transgression by adopting more stringent rules that are of a similar nature. By adhering to a more stringent rule that restricts women from reading the text in public – even though it is not actually necessary – the rabbi tries to ensure that no one breaks any actual rules. Charka issues two rejoinders to the rabbi's ruling. First, as an internal monologue, he draws awareness to the dangers of fence-building, which stem from the fact that every fence has two sides; while it is true that the fence protects the law, by placing women's opportunities to experience Jewish ritual on the opposite side of the fence, the rabbi is discounting their abilities to meaningfully engage with Jewish ritual and their feelings about being excluded from a religious experience. In the concluding panel of the comic, Charka offers an interpretation of the Purim story that he only recently realized. He explains to the rabbi that in communities where the leadership feels threatened by independent women, that same leadership will come to persecute the Jewish people in the future.[29] Read in isolation, Charka's statement can be understood as an opaque reference to the Purim story. There, the non-Jewish King Ahasuerus is insulted by his non-Jewish wife Vashti and eventually, under the aegis of his advisor Haman, he agrees to not only kill Vashti but to also exterminate the Jewish people.[30] Located within a comic that has already questioned religious rulings, Charka's holiday insight is a pointed attack against a religious leadership that prefers to silence the voices of empowered women than create space for their religious expression within Jewish communities. Charka is not advocating for an overhaul of religious tradition; his comments do, however, advance a progressive agenda within a traditional community wherein he disagrees with how rabbinic leaders use their authority to prioritize one value over another. As noted above, Charka's comics are unique within the Israeli comics landscape as he is the only settler with a national audience. His comics therefore gain power because of their presence and reach; Charka's willingness as a man to engage with and challenge the gendered hegemonies that have been established within his own religious community are no less disruptive than those discussed by any of the other artists considered in this study. Like them, Charka uses his voice and pen to call attention to the contrasting realities between the historic religious situation and the present reality and advocates for a change in which entrenched hegemonic positions are no longer tenable for the sustained growth and development of a religious Israeli community.

Lesbian excursions in Ilana Zeffren's "Zina" and "Holidays"

Tel Aviv resident Ilana Zeffren has been publishing comics in Israeli newspapers since 2006. Her first series, *Rishumon* (Urban Tails), was an autobiographical series that ran for seven years and was about her life in Tel Aviv as an out lesbian and the conversations that she had with her cats Spaghetti and Rafi. A collected volume was released by Pardes in 2014. Currently, she produces a weekly comic in the left-wing newspaper Haaretz about current events in Israeli society, told from Zeffren's and her cats' perspectives. In addition to her two weekly comics, Zeffren released *Pink Story* in 2004, a book-length graphic novel about the history of LGBTQ communities in Israel published by Mapa, and a few short stories which are freely accessible on her website. Aside from a few strips which have been translated into English, the majority of her work is only available in Hebrew, and as of this writing, *Pink Story* is only available for purchase directly from Zeffren on her Etsy store. While I will make reference to *Pink Story*, I have chosen to instead focus on two of Zeffren's short stories. These stories – "Zina" and "Holidays" – are more easily available for readers, given their presence on Zeffren's website, and when considered together, the themes and topics that they address cover many of the same ones that are found in *Pink Story*.

Among all of the authors and texts considered in this study, Zeffren's work is both the most liberal and the most political. This is because homosexuality is a highly charged topic within Israeli society and much of Zeffren's work directly engages with her sexual identity in relation to Israeli attitudes towards the LGBTQ community. A consistent theme that runs throughout her work is the need to normalize homosexual relationships within Israeli society despite the religious and political bodies that attempt to either eliminate any homosexual presence from the public sphere or to relegate it to the periphery of society. Israel inherited anti-sodomy laws from the British when it declared independence in 1948, and despite a Supreme Court verdict in 1963 that consenting adults could not be prosecuted for homosexual acts, same-sex relationships were not legalized until 1988. While Tel Aviv is considered by many to be one of the gay capitals of the world and Israel is recognized as being invariably more progressive than many of its neighboring countries, LGBTQ members do not share the same access to Israeli society as heterosexual Israelis. LGBTQ Israelis are unable to legally wed in Israel because marriage falls under the purview of the state's religious bodies, none of whom will officiate at same-sex unions. Furthermore, as Alon Raab points out, Zeffren "has grown up in a society where sexual identity is well defined and limited, any deviation from the norm is contested".[31] Zeffren's normalization of the LGBTQ community is most noticeably evident in her series *Rishumon*. There, she does not justify her gay identity or even engage with it in most of the weekly comics; instead, her relationship with her partner just is. There are no introductions or polemics about why they are together. Instead, their relationship is normalized to the point of it not being a topic worth discussing. Far more interesting to Zeffren are all of their weekly experiences, and these are the subjects that Zeffren actually wants to write about. Moving past her sexuality as her primary identity marker allows the reader to gain a more complete and comprehensive understanding of her life.

The opportunities and limitations for full inclusion in Israeli society for LGBTQ Israelis is made readily apparent in a short fictional comic called "Zina" that Zeffren published on her website. A young mid-twenties lesbian named Gabriella is saddened by a recent breakup and laments the emotional vulnerability that relationships entail. She wishes that she could have sex without any strings attached, but all of the lesbians she knows want relationships. This leads her to wonder whether there are any lesbian prostitutes in Israel and, much to her surprise, she finds in the phonebook the number for Ziva, a lesbian prostitute whose professional name is Zina.[32] Gabriella chooses to call her, and they subsequently engage in casual sex. The opportunity for same-sex prostitution to be advertised in the phonebook is indicative of a society that is progressive and willing to tolerate homosexuality. Yet the reader comes to learn that not only is Ziva the only lesbian prostitute in Tel Aviv, but Gabriella is the first person to ever call her. Moreover, even though she initially refused to re-enter a relationship, within a week Gabriella and Ziva are a couple, and within a month Gabriella has moved in to Ziva's apartment. The speed at which the relationship progresses – especially given their initial meeting as prostitute and client, alongside Gabriella's refusal to recouple – testifies to the complex landscape for out lesbians in Israeli society and the challenges they face in finding each other. For while Tel Aviv might have an active nightlife and hosts one of the world's largest pride festivals, for actual members of the community, navigating daily life is not so simple, nor is finding a partner to build a home with.

Much of Zeffren's work is a counterclaim to the hegemonic narrative that situates homosexuals as outside of the pale of normative Israeli society. In the concluding panel of "Zina", Gabriella is shown birthing a cat from her vagina for her and Ziva. The absurdity of the situation belies the uncomfortable reality under which lesbians live in Israel. If the role of the woman is to birth the future soldiers and mothers of the state, lesbians are unable to participate in the role that has been ascribed to them. Zeffren's illustration of a difficult and painful labor followed by the arrival of a new cat casts aspersions on the ways that Israeli society has commodified women's bodies and denied lesbians equal access to notions of femininity. When Gabriella gives birth to a cat and establishes her own family with cats as surrogates for children, Zeffren powerfully challenges the national narrative that denies lesbian couples space in the country's cultural tapestry. Instead, new notions of family are needed for Israelis – regardless of sexual orientation – who do not want to subscribe to the hegemonic familial narrative that prioritizes children as the rationale for coupling. At the same time that she offers a new understanding of the lesbian community's place in Israeli society, Zeffren does reaffirm traditional notions of femininity through her rapid recoupling.[33] Despite her initial interest in exploring the singles scene, her partnering with Zina reaffirms the notion that Israeli women are expected to be in committed relationships. The disconnect between her simultaneous rejection and adoption of Israeli feminine norms ultimately reaffirms the notion that – like other Israeli women – Israeli lesbians also feel pulled in a number of directions and must find ways to navigate these tensions in ways that best meet their individual needs.

"Zina" also introduces the reader to some of the many ways that Zeffren embeds visual coding into her comics in order to produce a more nuanced and complex reading of Israeli society. Silvia Adler and Galia Yanoshevsky have astutely pointed out that Zeffren's use of the peripheries and margins of her pages "draws the reader's attention to elements otherwise missing from the center".[34] The drawing away from the center operates on both a literal and metaphoric way. In "Zina", Zeffren frequently makes use of differently shaped heart emojis; these different shapes inform the reader of Gabriella's emotions and provide insight into how she is feeling and processing her experiences. Some are obvious and banal – like the large X through a heart accompanying her statement that she doesn't want a relationship – while others are more nuanced. For example, accompanying an image of Gabriella knocking on Ziva's door for the first time is a heart with a question-mark in the center and ellipses framing the heart on both sides. The combination of the trembling heart alongside the question mark is suggestive of the anxiety and excitement that Gabriella is feeling as she is about to pay for sex for the first time in her life. Despite her bravado and confidence at wanting sex with no feelings, this heart emoji is indicative of feelings of insecurity at embarking on a new type of relationship. Like many other features of Zeffren's comics, by virtue of being hidden on the outskirts of panels and in the white spaces between them, the hearts are reflective of the ways that LGBTQ Israelis also operate on the fringes of Israeli society. The inclusion of significant details in the margins similarly testifies to the importance of LGBTQ Israelis as part of the fabric of Israeli society and rejects notions of irrelevance. Despite being relegated to the sidelines, their experiences are valuable and contribute to the diversity of Israeli life, but this is only accessible for those who are willing to look and find meaning outside of the mainstream. Elsewhere, speech bubbles push through the panel's borders, forcing the reader to think and read outside of the box. These artistic details are symbolic of the ways that Zeffren uses her medium to push against the status quo and to demand noticing.

Throughout, features like the hearts draw the reader into the work, facilitating an opportunity to begin to think about Israeli society anew. Elsewhere in "Zina", Zeffren requires the reader to turn the page upside down in order to read Ziva's advertisement. The ad is illustrated facing Gabriella as she sits on the toilet, seeking out a prostitute. In order to read the advertisement, the reader must turn the comic 180 degrees in order to learn about Ziva's services. Engaging the reader in this way creates an immersive experience that engages the reader in Gabriella's discovery of the only lesbian prostitute in the area. It allows the reader to see the page through Gabriella's eyes – if only for a moment – and to experience the excitement that she feels as she comes to realize that her fantasy can come true.

By focusing on her story and the LGBTQ story, Zeffren repositions homosexuality in Israel away from the margins and into the center. This doesn't mean that homosexuality replaces heterosexuality, but the virtual absence of heterosexual relationships in her works testifies to an alternative Israel that exists away from what most Israelis experience. By telling her story as an Israeli story, Zeffren is illustrating an Israel that is more inclusive towards non-hegemonic relationships. Highlighting the lives of Israel's lesbians shines a light on their stories, moving them away from the margins and introducing their stories to wider Israeli society.

At the same time that Zeffren is staking a claim in the public sphere for LGBTQ Israelis, she also exhibits self-awareness, which allows her to recognize that her vision for Israeli society is neither normative nor accepted by all. A visual trope that Zeffren uses throughout much of her work in order to call attention to the ways that she and other LGBTQ Israelis are different is by illustrating horns on their heads (Figure 3.4). Shaded in pink, the horns symbolize the ways that Zeffren comes to recognize her non-hegemonic identity within Israeli society. Ofra Amihay locates in the triangular horns a prideful reappropriation of the pink triangles that homosexuals were required to wear by the Nazis.[35] I see in the pink horns a subtle awareness of her differences alongside a willingness to reject the negative associations between homosexuals and sinners. The horns are a playful attempt to reckon with the difficulty of simultaneously wanting to be fully integrated into Israeli society alongside a recognition that aspects of her identity are not yet considered normative and that therefore full inclusion in Israeli society is not an option at the present.

Figure 3.4 Zeffren with pink horns. Credit: Ilana Zeffren, *Pink Story*, (Tel Aviv: Mapa, 2005), 129.

It is perhaps in the sphere of religious life where Zeffren most clearly demonstrates her difficulty assimilating into Jewish-Israeli society. Even though she and her partner are secular Tel Aviv Israelis, avoiding Judaism is impossible for Zeffren on both personal and national levels. These tensions are made manifestly clear in her autobiographical comic "Moadim" (Holidays) that is available on her website. The story contains three short vignettes, with each corresponding to one of the three biblical holiday pilgrimages Jews were expected to make to Jerusalem on a yearly basis. In the first short story, instead of travelling to Jerusalem, Zeffren and her partner travel to the northern city of Zefat, where her partner's religious parents live. Zeffren and her partner dress modestly, being respectful of the city's traditional community. Upon arrival, they are gifted books of religious scriptures and a sermon about biblical verses outlining the subordinate role ascribed to women in Jewish tradition by her partner's parents. The following day, they attend synagogue for the holiday of Simhat Torah. Like most Israeli synagogues, men and women sit separately. Zeffren illustrates the women's section gridded with prison-like bars, relegating the women to spectators as they cheer on the dancing men in the holier space that they occupy with the Torah scrolls. In the second pilgrimage, Zeffren experiences further humiliation right before the holiday of Passover when she is prevented from visiting her partner's hospital room following an operation. This is because they are unwed, and, much to her horror, her partner's Orthodox stepfather is granted first visitation because he is a rabbi. In a move that is both painful and offensive, Zeffren is repeatedly encouraged to pretend to be her partner's sister and not her girlfriend, as this would permit her entrance to the room. Eventually granted an audience with her partner, Zeffren is dismayed at how no one is willing to recognize the legitimacy of their union.

"Holidays" exemplifies the complex relationship that Zeffren navigates as a Jewish-Israeli lesbian. While entirely secular, her life still involves religious aspects not only because of her partner's parents, but because of the ways that religion operates within Israeli society. The comic is reflective of Heike Bauer's assertion that Zeffren "takes the lesbian everyday as the starting point for exploring other issues".[36] In the case of "Holidays", Zeffren uses her personal experiences as an opportunity to critique the relationship between religion and society in Israel. Her comic testifies to the reality that, even for secular Israelis, religion is a significant determiner in daily life. This is evident in the ways that Zeffren chooses to mark time in her relationship according to the Jewish holidays. At the start of each mini-story, Zeffren notes both the holiday being celebrated and the length of her relationship with her girlfriend. Presenting time in a way that is dependent on the Jewish holiday cycle is reflective of the very religious worldview that Zeffren dismisses. Within the comic, she is unable to participate in the Simhat Torah celebrations because she is a woman, and she openly shares that if not for her partner's mother, their apartment would not have any food prepared for the Passover holiday. The act of opting out of Jewish rituals while simultaneously calling attention to them is indicative of the complexities of daily life that many secular Israelis experience while living in a Jewish country. For Zeffren, these complexities are heightened even further because of the personal connection to traditional Judaism and the national barriers that limit her full access to society. Writing about *Pink Story*, Zeffren's full-length graphic memoir about the history of LGBTQ communities in Israel and her own coming-out story, Raab notes that Zeffren "commemorates hitherto voiceless communities and offers a more intimate account of the individual's sense of identity and belonging".[37] The repeated encourage-ment to hide her relationship by pretending to be her partner's sister and not her lover is indicative of a society that has not yet normalized same-sex relationships. Yet in a testament to her moral fortitude and deter-mination to proudly claim her identity as an out Jewish-Israeli lesbian, Zeffren refuses to pretend to be who she is not; she insists that their rela-tionship is as legitimate as any other in the state. The familial experiences of religious holiday celebrations that her partner's parents try to include them in reinforce the ways that the state limits Zeffren from being able to create her own familial experiences in whichever way she would want. Judaism and Jewish tradition thus comes to serve as a barrier and gate-keeper, enabling access to some while limiting access to others, all the while being a presence in all of Israel's citizens' lives. By reaffirming her relationship, Zeffren challenges the religious and national foundations and carves out a space where she and her partner can exist together irre-spective of societal expectations.

The comics considered in this chapter introduce far more progres-sive, aggressive, and non-hegemonic voices than those presented in the earlier chapters and are essential voices for understanding the evolu-tion of the Israeli graphic novel. These works normalize the ways that religious nationalists, immigrants, and gays and lesbians become part of Israeli society and change its fabric. Raab has written that in Ilana Zeffren's work

> gays and lesbians are thus portrayed not only as sexual beings but also as "normal" people – an obvious message but one still not accepted by all Israelis, perhaps because it runs so counter to Zionist norms of masculinity and femininity.[38]

The same is equally true about all of the works considered in this chapter. Whether it is Charka's humor or Kichka's protests, regular and average Israelis living their regular and average lives itself is a challenge to the national mythology of the Israeli as hero. Telling the stories of the average Israelis who, alongside their challenges to gender norms, also have rich and meaningful lives is a crucial part of the twenty-first century Israeli story. As the country becomes even more established, the stories of regular Israelis whose autobiographies were not forged by war will become even more essential in the deconstruction of hegemonic gender roles. This process can be powerfully accomplished by sharing and telling the stories of everyday Israel and the loves and losses felt by different members of Israeli society.

Notes

1 The absence of these characters is significantly less evident in other forms of literature and in film. In the past 20 years, a number of Israeli authors have received acclaim for their work focusing on minority communities. In 2000, Haim Sabato, an Orthodox Jew, won the Sapir Prize for Best Israeli Novel for his book *Adjusting Sights*, which is set during the 1973 Yom Kippur War and in which the protagonist Haim navigates his dual identities as a soldier and a religiously observant Israeli. Much like Sabato's work, recent Israeli television programs have also become increasingly centered on the lives of traditional Jews. These include the coming-of-age stories told in *Shtisel* and *A Touch Away*, which won multiple awards at the Israeli Film Academy's Ophir Awards. Israeli and international prizes have also been awarded to books that present the experiences of non-Jews who come to Israel on religious pilgrimages and non-Jewish migrant workers who work in Israeli industries. A.B. Yehoshua's *A Woman in Jerusalem* won the 2006 LA Times Book of the Year for the ways that it interrogated Israeli society's loss of humanity in the wake of Palestinian suicide bombings and how an anonymous non-Israeli woman's body went unclaimed in a city morgue following a terror attack. Merav Nakar-Sadi's *Oxana* similarly questions the ways that Israelis have become habituated to injustices in their society. Focusing on the plight of migrant workers, Nakar-Sadi's book won the Sapir Prize in 2014 for Best New Author. Notable examples of Palestinian-Arab citizens of Israel who have received local and international acclaim for their work as poets, authors, and television writers include Samih al-Qasim, whose poetry has been translated into many languages, and Sayed Kashua, the most prominent Palestinian-Arab writer alive today. Kashua was the writer of the popular television program *Arab Labor*, a weekly columnist about Arab society for the Israeli newspaper *Haaretz* and a writer whose semi-autobiographical fiction has been awarded the Bernstein Prize, a prize for the best Israeli work by writers 50 years old and younger. While still a

relatively young Israeli community, a number of noteworthy texts have been produced by Ethiopian authors, including Shimuel Yelma, Omri Tegamlak Avera, and Dalia Betolin-Sherman. Lastly, producing works that feature and depict LGBTQ characters and relationships is increasingly losing its status as taboo in Israeli society. One of the earliest novels was Yossi Avni's *The Four Sons*, which explores sexual identity as part of a society that was still structured around heteronormative constructions of masculinity. While same-sex relationships are significantly less prevalent in Israeli media than in other Western countries, a number of films produced since 2000 have included gay characters, and not only in token roles. Most notable among the community of gay Israeli filmmakers is Eytan Fox, whose films include *Yossi and Jagger*, *Walk on Water*, and *The Bubble*, all of which were popular with both the LGBTQ and heterosexual Israeli communities.

2 Serraf, "Holocaust Impiety in 21st Century Graphic Novels", 5.
3 Kichka, *Falafel with Hot Sauce*, 47.
4 Kichka, *Falafel with Hot Sauce*, 57.
5 Kichka, *Falafel with Hot Sauce*, 19.
6 Kichka, *Falafel with Hot Sauce*, 83.
7 Many of the comics are also freely available on Charka's website. To help the interested reader, I have provided citations that link to the comics on the website in the bibliography.
8 Known in Israel as *dati-leumi*, religious nationalists are a community of Orthodox Jews who also support Israel as a Zionist and democratic state. Unlike secular Jewish Israelis, who are not regularly engaged in the observance of Jewish law, and also unlike the majority of ultra-Orthodox (*haredi*) Israeli Jews, who do not serve in the army or participate in Israel's political system, *dati-leumi* Israelis are defined by their commitment to both Zionist and religious enterprises. In general, religious-nationalist Israelis can be characterized by a number of core values. These include a belief in the sanctity of the land of Israel because it was given to the Jewish people by God in the Torah, a support for the Israeli government, a commitment to serving in the army, a strong interest in settling all of the biblical land of Israel (especially in the West Bank), and an opposition to ceding territory to Palestinians for a future Palestinian state.
9 Charka, "Superhero".
10 Charka, "The Dirty Laundry".
11 Charka, "Impressions".
12 Charka, "Tel Aviv".
13 Lubell, "Israeli Military Struggles".
14 Eglash, "Netanyahu's Plan".
15 Readers can see the myriad differences between the communities in the 2016 Pew Research Center's publication *Israel's Religiously Divided Society*.
16 McCloud, *Understanding Comics*, 46.
17 Charka, "Favourite Son".
18 When Israelis vote in national elections, they use a ballot with a 1–3 letter abbreviation or word chosen by the party written upon it. This word is

written in a large font and it is only in smaller letters underneath that the party's full name is written. The large letters allow voters to easily identify the party that they want to vote for.

19 Charka, "Creative World".
20 Charka, "On the Line".
21 Charka, "Prejudices".
22 Charka, "Tact".
23 Charka, "Opposing Interests".
24 Charka, "Aftershock".
25 Chute, *Disaster Drawn*, 36.
26 Chute, *Disaster Drawn*, 141–142.
27 Charka, "Superhero".
28 Bell, "Settler Cartoonist Shay Charka".
29 Charka, "Women's Reading". I am grateful to Assaf Gamzou for his help in translating this comic.
30 While the story says that Vashti is banished, the clear subtext is that she was killed.
31 Raab, "Ben Gurion's Golem", 225.
32 Zina is a play on the Hebrew word "Zona", which is a female prostitute who solicits male clients. The nuance of this is lost in translation.
33 I am grateful to Alexandria Silver for pointing out this idea about Zeffren's decision to begin a committed relationship so soon after the previous one ended and how it reaffirms traditional Israeli gender norms.
34 Adler and Yanoshevsky, "Center and Periphery", 92.
35 Amihay, "Red Diapers, Pink Stories", 51.
36 Bauer, "Graphic Lesbian Continuum", 98.
37 Raab, "Ben Gurion's Golem", 214.
38 Raab, "Ben Gurion's Golem", 229.

Conclusion

Matt Reingold

Coming from a country that is not yet 75 years old, Israel's comics and cartooning tradition is relatively young. Before Israel's birth in 1948, Batman and Superman were already protecting Gotham City and Metropolis, Captain America had already fought in World War II, and Tintin had travelled around the world with his furry companion Snowy. Situated in the Middle East, Israelis were also not surrounded by countries with a rich tradition of writing and illustrating graphic narratives.

Despite a relatively late start, by the beginning of the twenty-first century, a mere 50 years after the country's birth, an established community of writers and illustrators who would tell uniquely Israeli stories in the form of comics and graphic novels was present. As part of a national community of writers and artists who critique society through the creative arts, Israeli graphic novelists offer new perspectives on Israeli society through the synthesis of word and image.

The central thesis of this book is that Israeli graphic novelists and cartoonists use their craft to visualize alternative Israels that position gender anew. Their works reify Marjorie C. Allison's observation that

> by seeing and reading themselves into the story, readers can actively reimagine how the world is constructed and how they are similar to and different from the world the writers present. What has been marginalized is brought to the centre and given a privileged place in these stories.[1]

The creation of different realities fosters new awareness of the limitations of hegemonic cultural constructs and facilitates thinking about the future of Israeli society in new ways. Considered together, the graphic novels explored in this volume offer a number of specific observations of, and recommendations for, Israeli society.

DOI: 10.4324/9781003150435-5

First, many of the graphic novels considered in this book suggest that the military has shaped understandings of gender in Israeli society and that the experiences of male and female soldiers are fundamentally different. Despite very different desired outcomes, a commonality of the writers and artists discussed here is a consistent critique of gender norms that have been fashioned by the IDF. Soldiers who reinforce the hegemony – like those who wantonly destroy Palestinian villages in *Farm 54* and who punch Israeli citizens in *Beyond the Line* – are depicted in a negative fashion. Conversely, soldiers who reflect on their complicity with unethical orders, like in Ari Folman and David Polonsky's *Waltz with Bashir*, and soldiers who refuse to blindly follow orders, like the Kichkas in *Falafel with Hot Sauce*, emphasize the importance of making sensitivity and compassion a core component of a soldier's values. Additionally, the depictions of female soldiers involve expanding the role and purview of women in the IDF from how they have traditionally been treated in the army. This includes Noga's revulsion at having to serve as a mother to a group of soldiers in *Farm 54*, Mica's job as a Krav Maga instructor in *The Property*, and even Numi's station as a soldier serving in the IDF during the Second Intifada in *Exit Wounds*. These female soldiers reject normative constructions of women as either outliers or caregivers and instead suggest that gender should not determine a soldier's station in the military.

Second, Israeli graphic novels offer a nuanced portrait of relationships as complex sites where individuals of both genders navigate rich histories in order to engage in meaningful partnerships. The relationships depicted – like the interfaith romance between Mica and Tomasz in *The Property*, and the homosexual connections between Gabriella and Ziva and Zeffren and her partner in Zeffren's "Zina" and "Holidays" – reject traditional Israeli attitudes towards endogamy and heterosexuality and instead recognize the ways that twenty-first century relationships expand the purview of traditional attitudes towards romance. More subtly, authors like Modan in *Exit Wounds* and *The Property*, Keret and Hanuka in *Pizzeria Kamikaze*, the Seliktars in *Farm 54*, and Hanuka in "The Realist" challenge traditional gendered relationship dichotomies in which men are expected to be strong and assertive and women are docile. To varying degrees, these texts include men who are either sensitive and in touch with their emotions or assertive and comfortable identifying their desires. These depictions reject traditional models of how men and women should behave in relationships and offer alternative – and more realistic – ways of being.

Third, in a similar vein to these romantic relationships, the depictions of parent–child relationships also eschew classic models of gendered child-rearing. Whether in the case of a man racing to get home to be with his children, like Asaf Hanuka in "The Realist", or Michel Kichka helping his sister take care of her newborn or being proud of the political stances his sons take in *Falafel with Hot Sauce*, the men in Israeli graphic novels are not relegated to the sidelines and they play a significant role in child-rearing. They are physically present and emotionally available for their children.

As a visual medium, comics and graphic novels are powerful tools that facilitate reader identification with characters. By introducing visual challenges to normative constructs of gender, readers of Israeli graphic novels are able to recognize a world that is similar to their own, yet not identical. Being able to see a world that is similar to but not the same as their own allows for reflection about which world is more ideal. This near-reality affords the reader an element of distance from present realities and allows for contemplative meditation on which is preferred. Graphic novels with complex characters who challenge national gendered mythologies can help change Israeli society and craft a new national narrative.

In Chapter 3, I discussed graphic novels that feature characters and topics that have been absent in the majority of Israeli graphic novels. It is important to recognize that despite the existence of a graphic novel featuring a lesbian or an Orthodox Jew, characters from these communities are a rarity in Israeli graphic novels, with only a few examples of LGBTQ characters in Ilana Zeffren's work, Mizrahim in Hanuka's comics, and religious characters in Shay Charka's comics. It is also worth pointing out that all of the authors, texts, and main characters, excluding Charka and his family, comfortably fit onto the left side of the Israeli political spectrum, with right-wing characters like Tamara in *Farm 54* serving mostly as props to buttress left-wing discourse. The absence of characters and creators from other segments of Israeli society in Israeli graphic novels is a sobering reminder that despite being a progressive genre, comics have not been democratized among Israeli citizenry and are still primarily made by heterosexual non-religious Jewish Israelis. I want to avoid holding Hanuka, Zeffren, and Charka up as evidence of significant progress and evolution because the publication of three or four texts that feature minority communities is not very considerable. There is still much to be done in these communities alongside the need to publish stories from the Ethiopian, Palestinian-Arab-Israeli, former Soviet Union, and ultra-Orthodox communities whose voices have not been heard. The absence of these characters in texts is reflective of a greater divide within Israeli society wherein certain communities – especially the ultra-Orthodox and Palestinian-Arab – are siloed, with limited interactions between them and the rest of Israeli society.[2]

As of this writing in winter 2021, new Hebrew-language graphic novels by Asaf Hanuka and Rutu Modan were just released that more directly grapple with some of the topics and issues that had not until then been featured in Israeli graphic novels. Hanuka's autobiographical series *The Jewish Arab* is a multigenerational narrative of his family's history and is the first mainstream comic told from a Mizrahi-Israeli perspective. In it, Hanuka reckons with his complex relationship with his own identity, as a Jew by religion, an Israeli by nationality, and an Arab by ethnicity. As well, Modan's *MiNaharot* (Tunnels) is her first graphic novel to be published first in Hebrew, with the English release not due until September 2021. The text includes a same-sex interfaith international relationship between an Israeli man and a Palestinian man, and a single-parent family. In addition to these books, Karina Shor, an Israeli born in Moldova, will be releasing *Silence, Full Stop: A Memoir* in late 2021. The text is noteworthy for being the first Israeli graphic novel to tell the story of a Jew who arrived from the former Soviet Union. It is also the first to address sexual assault, as Shor recounts the story of her own childhood abuse and its impact on her life in subsequent years. Together, these three texts interrogate topics and communities that had previously not been addressed by Israeli graphic novelists, and therefore represent important evolutions in the subject matter of Israeli graphic novels.

It is my hope that these texts herald a new wave of Israeli graphic novels that truly reflect the diversity of Israeli society and introduce readers to the perspectives and experiences of communities that have not yet had their stories told. The uniqueness of these communities means that each possesses its own gender dynamics with as-yet untold stories. Their inclusion in the catalogue of Israeli graphic novels will allow for an even richer and more nuanced understanding of the complexities of Israeli society and will more accurately depict the diversity of the Israeli people.

Notes

1 Allison, "(Not) Lost in the Margins", 74.
2 I am thankful to Assaf Gamzou for helping with the development of this paragraph.

Bibliography

A Touch Away. Tel Aviv: Reshet, 2007.

Actus Comics. *Summer Love*. Tel Aviv: Actus Independent Comics, 2007.

Adler, Silvia, and Galia Yanoshevsky. "Center and Periphery in Ilana Zeffren's Autobiographical Graphic Novel *Pink Story* (2005)." In *The Representation of the Relationship between Center and Periphery in the Contemporary Novel*, edited by Ruth Amer and Françoise Saquer-Sabin, 86–98. Newcastle upon Tyne: Cambridge Scholars Publishing, 2018.

Ahronheim, Anna. "A Third of Israeli Youth Do Not Enlist in the IDF." *Jerusalem Post*. January 19, 2020. www.jpost.com/israel-news/half-of-israeli-youth-do-not-enlist-in-idf-614604.

Allison, Marjorie C. "(Not) Lost in the Margins: Gender and Identity in Graphic Texts." *Mosaic* 47, no. 4 (2014): 73–97. www.jstor.com/stable/44030722.

Amihay, Ofra. "Red Diapers, Pink Stories: Color Photography and Self-Outing in Jewish Women's Comics." *Image & Narrative* 16, no. 2 (2015): 42–64. www.imageandnarrative.be/index.php/imagenarrative/article/view/811.

Avni-Levy, Yossi. *The Four Sons*. Modi'in: Zmora-Bitan, 1998.

Barron, Melody. "The Comic Books on the Ultra-Orthodox Bookshelf." *The Librarians*. June 28, 2018. https://blog.nli.org.il/en/haredi_comics/.

Bauer, Helke. "Graphic Lesbian Continuum: Ilana Zeffren." In *Graphic Details: Jewish Women's Confessional Comics in Essays and Interviews*, edited by Sarah Lightman, 98–109. Jefferson, NC: McFarland & Company, Inc., Publishers, 2014.

Bell, Matthew. "Settler Cartoonist Shay Charka Skewers All Sectors of Israeli Society." *The World*. January 13, 2012. www.pri.org/stories/2012-01-13/settler-cartoonist-shay-charka-skewers-all-sectors-israeli-society.

Biale, David. *Eros and the Jews: From Biblical Israel to Contemporary America*. Berkeley: University of California Press, 1992.

Blumen, Orna, and Sharon Halevi. "Staging Peace through a Gendered Demonstration: Women in Black in Haifa, Israel." *Annals of the Association of American Geographers* 99, no. 5 (2009): 977–985. www.jstor.com/stable/20621267.

Boyarin, Daniel. *Unheroic Conduct: The Rise of Heterosexuality and the Invention of the Jewish Man.* Berkeley: University of California Press, 1997.

Brown, Hannah. "Topless Protest Outside Knesset Sparks Social Media Storm." *The Jerusalem Post.* July 22, 2020. www.jpost.com/israel-news/shameless-protest-by-topless-woman-sparks-social-media-storm-635959.

Buchweitz, Nurit. "Vitalities and Fatalities in Intimate Relationships in Etgar Keret's Graphic Narratives." In *Intimate Relationships in Cinema, Literature and Visual Culture,* edited by Gilad Padva and Nurit Buchweitz, 37–48. Cham, Switzerland: Palgrave Macmillan, 2017.

Calcalist. "Who is the Big Winner." July 4 201. www.calcalist.co.il/articles/0,7340,L-3716325,00.html.

Carmit Yefet, Karin. "Feminism and Hyper-Masculinity in Israel: A Case Study in Deconstructing Legal Fatherhood." *Yale Journal of Law and Feminism* 27, no. 1 (2015): 47–94.

Castel-Bloom, Orly. *Dolly City.* Chicago: Dalkey Archive Press, 2010.

Charka, Shay. *Beyond the Line.* Moshav Ben Shemen: Modan, 2008.

Charka, Shay. "Favourite Son." October 5, 2009. http://shaycharka.blogspot.com/2009/10/2-2.html.

Charka, Shay. "On the Line." October 27, 2009. http://shaycharka.blogspot.com/2009/10/2-5.html.

Charka, Shay. "Impressions." Translated by Robbie Gringras. November 22, 2009. http://shaycharka.blogspot.com/2009/11/translations.html.

Charka, Shay. "Prejudices." Translated by Robbie Gringras. November 22, 2009. http://shaycharka.blogspot.com/2009/11/translations.html.

Charka, Shay. "The Dirty Laundry." Translated by Robbie Gringras. November 22, 2009. http://shaycharka.blogspot.com/2009/11/translations.html.

Charka, Shay. "Creative World." November 24, 2009. http://shaycharka.blogspot.com/2009/11/2-9.html.

Charka, Shay. "Opposing Interests." January 19, 2010. http://shaycharka.blogspot.com/2010/01/2-17.html.

Charka, Shay. "Aftershock." January 26, 2010. http://shaycharka.blogspot.com/2010/01/2-18.html.

Charka, Shay. "Women's Reading." March 9, 2010. http://shaycharka.blogspot.com/2010/03/2-24.html.

Charka, Shay. "Tel Aviv." March 16, 2010. http://shaycharka.blogspot.com/2010/03/2-25.html.

Charka, Shay. "Superhero." April 14, 2010. http://shaycharka.blogspot.com/2010/04/2-29.html.

Charka, Shay. "Tact." April 19, 2010. http://shaycharka.blogspot.com/2010/04/2-30.html.

Charka, Shay. *Beyond the Line: Outside the Lines.* Moshav Ben Shemen: Modan, 2012.

Chute, Hillary L. *Disaster Drawn: Visual Witness, Comics, and Documentary Form.* Cambridge, MA: The Belknap Press of Harvard University, 2016.

Delisle, Guy. *Jerusalem: Chronicles from the Holy City.* Montreal: Drawn & Quarterly, 2011.

Devir, Yehuda, and Maya Devir. *One of These Days*. New York: Random House, 2020.

Dreifuss, Maya, dir. *She's Coming Home*. Israel: Lama Hafakot and Metro Tikshoret, 2014.

Economist. "Mission Unaccomplished: Binyamin Netanyahu Boasted Too Soon of Defeating the Coronavirus." July 25, 2020. www.economist.com/middle-east-and-africa/2020/07/23/binyamin-netanyahu-boasted-too-soon-of-defeating-the-coronavirus.

Eglash, Ruth. "Netanyahu's Plan for West Bank Annexation Faces Unexpected Opposition from Settlers." *Washington Post*. June 10, 2020. www.washingtonpost.com/world/middle_east/netanyahus-plan-for-west-bank-annexation-faces-unexpected-opposition-from-settlers/2020/06/10/9db6c694-a744-11ea-898e-b21b9a83f792_story.html.

Eshed, Eli. "Hebrew Comics – A History." December 24, 2003. https://no666.wordpress.com/2003/12/24/hebrew-comics-a-history/.

Eshed, Eli, and Uri Fink. *HaGolem: Sipuro Shel Comics Israeli*. Tel Aviv: Modan, 2003.

Esteron, Yoel, Galit Hemi, and Gabi Kessler. "About Calcalist." *Calcalist*. www.calcalist.co.il/home/0,7340,L-3854,00.html.

Folman, Ari, and David Polonsky. *Waltz with Bashir*. New York: Metropolitan Books, 2009.

Folman, Ari, and David Polonsky. *Anne Frank's Diary: The Graphic Adaptation*. New York: Pantheon, 2018.

Fox, Eytan, dir. *Yossi and Jagger*. Tel Aviv: Lama Films, 2002.

Fox, Eytan, dir. *Walk on Water*. Tel Aviv: Lama Films, 2004.

Fox, Eytan, dir. *The Bubble*. Tel Aviv: Uchovsky Fox, 2006.

Frenkel, Michal. "Reprogramming Femininity? The Construction of Gender Identities in the Israeli Hi-tech Industry between Global and Local Gender Orders." *Gender, Work and Organization* 15, no. 4 (2008): 352–374. https://doi.org/10.1111/j.1468-0432.2008.00398.x.

Fuchs, Esther. "Gender, War, and Zionist Mythogynies: Feminist Trends in Israeli Scholarship." In *Narratives of Dissent: War in Contemporary Israeli Arts and Culture*, edited by Rachel S. Harris and Ranen Omer-Sherman, 264–278. Detroit: Wayne State University Press, 2012.

Gamzou, Assaf. "Third-Generation Graphic Syndrome: New Directions in Comics and Holocaust Memory in the Age after Testimony." *Journal of Holocaust Research* 33, no. 3 (2019): 224–237. https://doi.org/10.1080/25785648.2019.1631574.

Gilman, Sander L. "The Jewish Body: A 'Footnote'." *Bulletin of the History of Medicine* 64, no. 4 (1990): 588–602. www.jstor.com/stable/44443185.

Glidden, Sarah. *How to Understand Israel in 60 Days or Less*. Montreal: Drawn & Quarterly, 2016.

Grossman, David. *To the End of the Land*. New York: Vintage, 2011.

Hanuka, Asaf. "About." www.asafhanuka.com/about-1.

Hanuka, Asaf. *The Realist*. Los Angeles: Archaia, 2015.

Hanuka, Asaf (@RealistComics). "Local Wonder." Twitter, June 11, 2017.

Hanuka, Asaf. *The Realist: Plug and Play*. Los Angeles: Archaia, 2017.

Hanuka, Asaf. *The Jewish Arab*. Tel Aviv: Calcalist, 2020. https://newmedia. calcalist.co.il/musaf-calcalist/medorim-hanuca/index.html.

Hanuka, Asaf, Tomer Hanuka, and Boaz Lavie. *The Divine*. New York: First Second, 2015.

Harris, Rachel S. "Decay and Death: Urban Topoi in Literary Depictions of Tel-Aviv." *Israel Studies* 14 no. 3 (2009): 75–93. www.jstor.com/stable/30245873.

Harris, Rachel S. "Parallel Lives: Palestinian, Druze, and Jewish Women in Recent Israeli Cinema on the Conflict: Free Zone, Syrian Bride, and Lemon Tree." *Shofar* 32, no. 1 (2013): 79–102. www.jstor.org/stable/10.5703/shofar.32.1.79.

Harris, Rachel S. *An Ideological Death: Suicide in Israeli Literature*. Evanston, IL: Northwestern University Press, 2014.

Harris, Rachel S. *Warriors, Witches, Whores: Women in Israeli Cinema*. Detroit: Wayne State University Press, 2017.

Hauser, Orlee. "'We Rule the Base Because We're Few': 'Lone Girls' in Israel's Military." *Journal of Contemporary Ethnography* 40, no. 6 (2011): 623–651. https://doi.org/10.1177%2F0891241611412959.

Haworth, Kevin. *The Comics of Rutu Modan: War, Love and Secrets*. Jackson, MS: University of Mississippi Press, 2019.

Hertzog, Esther and Assaf Lev. "Male Dominance under Threat: Machoism Confronts Female Defiance in Israeli Gyms." *Journal of Contemporary Ethnography* 48, no. 6 (2019): 836–866. https://doi.org/10.1177%2F0891241619834662.

Hirsch, Dafna. "Hummus Masculinity in Israel." *Food, Culture & Society* 19, no. 2 (2016): 337–359. https://doi.org/10.1080/15528014.2016.1178550.

Hirsch, Dafna, and Dana Grosswirth Kachtan. "Is 'Hegemonic Masculinity' Hegemonic *as* Masculinity: Two Israeli Case Studies." *Men and Masculinities* 21, no. 5 (2018): 687–708. https://doi.org/10.1177/1097184X17696186.

Hollander, Philip. "Shifting Manhood: Masculinity and the Lebanon War in *Beaufort* and *Waltz with Bashir*." In *Narratives of Dissent: War in Contemporary Israeli Arts and Culture*, edited by Rachel S. Harris and Ranen Omer-Sherman, 346–363. Detroit: Wayne State University Press, 2012.

Jacobson, David C. "Intimate Relations between Israelis and Palestinians in Fiction by Israeli Women Writers." *Shofar* 25, no. 3 (2007): 32–46. www.jstor.com/stable/42944334.

Jacoby, Tami Amanda. *Women in Zones of Conflict: Gender Structures and Women's Resistance in Israel*. Montreal: McGill-Queen's University Press, 2005.

Jacoby, Tami Amanda. "Fighting in the Feminine: The Dilemmas of Combat Women in Israel." In *Gender, War, and Militarism: Feminist Perspectives*, edited by Laura Sjoberg and Sandra Via, 80–90. Santa Barbara, CA: Praeger, 2010.

Kahn, Ariel. "From Darkness into Light: Reframing Notions of Self and Other in Contemporary Israeli Graphic Narratives." In *The Jewish Graphic Novel: Critical Approaches*, edited by Samantha Baskind and Ranen Omer-Sherman, 198–213. New Brunswick, NJ: Rutgers University Press, 2008.

Kaplan, Danny. "The Military as a Second Bar Mitzvah: Combat Service as Initiation to Zionist Masculinity." In *Imagined Masculinities: Male Identity and Culture in the Modern Middle East*, edited by Emma Sinclair-Webb and Mai Ghoussoub, 127–144. London: Al-Saqi Books, 2000.

Kashua, Sayed, writer. *Arab Labor*. Jerusalem: Chanel 2 Keshet, 2007–2013.

Katsman, Roman. "Ishiyut, Etika ve-Ideologiya be-Mitopoesis ha-Postmoderni shel Etgar Keret." *Mi'kan* 4 (2005): 20–41.

Keret, Etgar, and Actus Comics. *Jetlag: Five Graphic Novellas*. New Milford, CT: The Toby Press, 1998.

Keret, Etgar, and Asaf Hanuka. *Pizzeria Kamikaze*. Los Angeles: Archaia, 2018.

Kichka, Michel. *Second Generation: The Things I Didn't Tell My Father*. Translated by Montana Kane. Paris: Europe Comics, 2016.

Kichka, Michel. *Falafel with Hot Sauce*. Translated by Montana Kane. Paris: Europe Comics, 2019.

Knell, Yolande. "Netanyahu Focus of Israeli Protests Against 'The King'." *BBC News*. August 15, 2020. www.bbc.com/news/world-middle-east-53724095.

Kroha, Lucienne. *The Drama of the Assimilated Jew: Giorgio Bassani's Romanzo di Ferrara*. Toronto: University of Toronto Press, 2013.

Lachover, Einat, Shosh Davidson, and Ornit Ramati Dvir. "The Authentic Conservative Wonder Woman: Israeli Girls Negotiating Global and Local Meanings of Femininity." *Celebrity Studies* (2009). https://doi.org/10.1080/19392397.2019.1691925.

Lambert, Josh. "Sex, Violence and Growing up on a Farm in Israel." *Forward*. July 1, 2011: 9–10.

Lehrer, Erica. "Can There be a Conciliatory Heritage?" *International Journal of Heritage Studies* 16, no. 4–5 (2010): 269–288. https://doi.org/10.1080/13527251003775596.

Levy, Moshe, Einat Hollander, and Smadar Noy-Canyon. "The Construction of Israeli 'Masculinity' in the Sports Arena." *Israel Affairs* 22, no. 2 (2016): 549–567. https://doi.org/10.1080/13537121.2016.1140351.

Lomsky-Feder, Edna, and Tamar Rapoport. "Juggling Models of Masculinity: Russian-Jewish Immigrants in the Israeli Army." *Sociological Inquiry* 73, no. 1 (2003): 114–137. https://doi.org/10.1111/1475-682X.00043.

Lubell, Maayan. "Israeli Military Struggles with Rising Influence of Religious-Zionists." *Reuters*. April 15, 2016. www.reuters.com/investigates/special-report/israel-military-religion/.

McCloud, Scott. *Understanding Comics: The Invisible Art*. New York: William Morrow, 1993.

Michel, Chantal Catherine. "Panels for Peace: Contributions of Israeli and Palestinian Comics to Peace-Building." *Quest* 5, (2013): 205–231. www.doi.org/10.48248/issn.2037-741X/765.

Modan, Rutu. *Exit Wounds*. Montreal: Drawn & Quarterly, 2007.

Modan, Rutu. "Homecoming." In *Jamilti and Other Stories*. Montreal: Drawn & Quarterly, 2008, 96–126.

Modan, Rutu. "Jamilti." In *Jamilti and Other Stories*. Montreal: Drawn & Quarterly, 2008, 6–17.

Modan, Rutu. *The Property*. Montreal: Drawn & Quarterly, 2013.

Modan, Rutu. *MiNaharot*. Moshav Ben-Shimon: Keter Books, 2020.

Munk, Yael. "From National Heroes to Postnational Witnesses: A Reconstruction of Israeli Soldiers' Cinematic Narratives as Witnesses of History." In *Narratives of Dissent: War in Contemporary Israeli Arts and Culture*, edited by Rachel S. Harris and Ranen Omer-Sherman, 300–316. Detroit: Wayne State University Press, 2012.

Murray, Ross. "The Feminine Mystique: Feminism, Sexuality, Motherhood." *Journal of Graphic Novels and Comics* 2, no. 1 (2011): 55–66. https://doi.org/ 10.1080/21504857.2011.576881.

Nakar-Sadi, Merav. *Oxana*. Tel Aviv: Ahuzat Bayit, 2013.

Oh, Stella. "Laughter Against Laughter: Interrupting Racial and Gendered Stereotypes in Gene Luen Yang's American Born Chinese." *Journal of Graphic Novels and Comics* 8, no. 1 (2017): 20–32. https://doi.org/10.1080/ 21504857.2016.1233897.

Oksman, Tahneer. *"How Come Boys Get to Keep Their Noses?": Women and Jewish American Identity in Contemporary Graphic Memoirs*. New York: Columbia University Press, 2016.

Olmert, Dana. "Mothers of Soldiers in Israeli Literature: The Return of the Politically Repressed." *Prooftexts* 33, no. 3 (2013): 333–364. www.jstor.org/ stable/10.2979/prooftexts.33.3.333.

Pekar, Harvey, and J.T. Waldman. *Not the Israel My Parents Promised Me*. New York: Hill and Wang, 2014.

Peled, Anat. "What Became of Tearful Ashdod Falafel Vendor, Symbol of COVID's Economic Toll." *Times of Israel*. July 9, 2020. www.timesofisrael. com/hard-up-falafel-vendor-who-came-to-symbolize-virus-economic-toll-reopens-store/.

Pew Research Center. *Israel's Religiously Divided Society*. 2006. www.pewforum. org/2016/03/08/israels-religiously-divided-society/.

Ploskov, Tali (@TaliPolskov). "Not like this...." Twitter, July 22, 2020.

Popper-Giveon, Ariela, Yael Keshet, and Ido Liberman. "Increasing Gender and Ethnic Diversity in the Health Care Workforce: The Case of Arab Male Nurses in Israel." *Nursing Outlook* 63, no. 6 (2015): 680–690. https://doi-org. ezproxy.library.yorku.ca/10.1016/j.outlook.2015.08.001.

Raab, Alon. "Ben Gurion's Golem and Jewish Lesbians: Subverting Hegemonic History in Two Israeli Graphic Novels." In *The Jewish Graphic Novel: Critical Approaches*, edited by Samantha Baskind and Ranen Omer-Sherman, 214–233. New Brunswick, NJ: Rutgers University Press, 2008.

Raz, Aviad E., and Gavan Tzruya. "Doing Gender in Segregated and Assimilative Organizations: Ultra-Orthodox Jewish Women in the Israeli High-Tech Labour Market." *Gender, Work & Organization* 25, no. 4 (2018): 361–378. https://doi.org/10.1111/gwao.12205.

Reingold, Matt. "Israeli and Polish Holocaust Commemoration in Rutu Modan's The Property." *The Journal of Holocaust Research* 33, no. 3 (2019): 175–190. https://doi.org/10.1080/25785648.2019.1627712.

Reingold, Matt. "A National Reckoning: Israeli Soldiers' Depictions of Wartime Trauma in Autobiographical Graphic Novels." *Journal of War & Culture Studies* (2019). https://doi.org/10.1080/17526272.2019.1689662.

Reingold, Matt. "Fantastical Autography in Asaf Hanuka's *The Realist.*" *Shofar* 38, no. 1 (2020): 146–166. https://muse.jhu.edu/article/753912.

Ronen, Shoshana. "Post-Holocaust Representations of Poland in Israeli Literature." *The Polish Review* 60, no. 3 (2015): 3–20. www.jstor.org/stable/10.5406/polishreview.60.3.0003.

Sabato, Haim. *Adjusting Sights.* Jerusalem: Toby Press, 2003.

Sacco, Joe. *Footnotes in Gaza.* New York: Metropolitan Books, 2010.

Sacco, Joe. *Palestine.* Seattle: Fantagraphics, 2014.

Sasson-Levy, Orna. "Constructing Identities at the Margins: Masculinities and Citizenship in the Israeli Army." *Sociological Quarterly* 43, no. 3 (2002): 357–383. https://doi.org/10.1111/j.1533-8525.2002.tb00053.x.

Sasson-Levy, Orna. "Military, Masculinity, and Citizenship: Tensions and Contradictions in the Experience of Blue-Collar Soldiers," *Identities: Global Studies in Culture and Power* 10 (2003): 319–345. https://doi.org/10.1080/10702890390228892.

Schwartz, Yigal. "The Person, the Path, and the Melody: A Brief History of Identity in Israeli Literature." *Prooftexts* 20, no. 3 (2000): 318–339. https://doi.org/10.1353/ptx.2000.0022.

Seliktar, Galit, and Gilad Seliktar, *Farm 54.* Wisbech, England: Fanfare/Ponent Mon, 2011.

Serraf, Lola. "Holocaust Impiety in 21st Century Graphic Novels: Younger Generations 'No Longer Obliged to Perpetuate Sorrow.'" *Genealogy* 3, no. 4 (2019): 1–13. https://doi.org/10.3390/genealogy3040053.

Shadmi, Koren. *The Abaddon.* New York: Z2 Comics, 2015.

Sharim, Yehuda. "Choreographing Masculinity in Contemporary Israeli Culture." In *Choreographies of 21st Century Wars*, edited by Gay Morris and Jens Richard Giersdorf, 133–156. Oxford: Oxford University Press, 2016.

Shiffman, Smadar. "'If not Now, When?': Israeli Literature and Political Responsibility." *Israel Studies Forum* 20, no. 1 (2005): 70–82. https://doi.org/10.3167/isf.2005.200105.

Shtisel. Netflix, 2013.

Sion, Liora, and Eyal Ben-Ari. "Imagined Masculinity: Body, Sexuality, and Family among Israeli Military Reserves." *Symbolic Interaction* 32, no. 1 (2009): 21–43. https://doi.org/10.1525/si.2009.32.1.21.

Spector-Mersel, Gabriela. "Never-aging Stories: Western Hegemonic Masculinity Scripts." *Journal of Gender Studies* 15, no.1 (2006): 67–82. https://doi.org/10.1080/09589230500486934.

Stadler, Nicolas, and Lea Taragin-Zeller. "Like a Snake in Paradise: Fundamentalism, Gender and Taboos in the Haredi Community." *Archives de Sciences-Sociales des Religions* 177 (2017): 133–156. https://doi.org/10.4000/assr.29300.

Tabachnick, Stephen E. "Strange Encounters in Rutu Modan's *Exit Wounds* and 'Jamilti'." In *Visualizing Jewish Narrative: Jewish Comics and Graphic*

Novels, edited by Derek Parker Royal, 231–240. London: Bloomsbury Academic, 2016.

Tabachnick, Stephen E. "The Jewish Graphic Novel." In *The Cambridge History of the Graphic Novel*, edited by Jan Baetens, Hugo Frey, and Stephen E. Tabachnick, 443–456. Cambridge: Cambridge University Press, 2018.

Times of Israel. "Topless Protester, a Social Work Student, Pushes Back Against Tide of Criticism." July 22, 2020. www.timesofisrael.com/topless-social-work-protester-pushes-back-against-tide-of-criticism/.

Times of Israel. "Israel's Virus-Battered Economy Sees Sharpest Contraction in 45 Years." August 16, 2020. www.timesofisrael.com/israels-virus-battered-economy-sees-sharpest-contraction-in-45-years/.

Weissbrod, Rachel, and Ayelet Kohn. "Collaborative Self-Translation – *Pizzeria Kamikaze* as a Case in Point." *Journal of Graphic Novels and Comics* 10, no. 4 (2019): 410–431. https://doi.org/10.1080/21504857.2018.1505647.

Whitlock, Gillian. "Autographics: The Seeing 'I' of the Comics." *MFS: Modern Fiction Studies* 52, no. 4 (2006): 965–979. https://doi.org/10.1353/mfs.2007.0013.

Whitlock, Gillian, and Anna Poletti. "Self-Regarding Art." *Biography* 31, no. 1 (2008): v–xxiii. www.jstor.org/stable/23540918.

Yakin, Boaz, and Nick Bertozzi. *Jerusalem: A Family Portrait*. New York: First Second, 2013.

Yang, Gene Luen. *American Born Chinese*. New York: First Second, 2006.

Yehoshua, A.B. *A Woman in Jerusalem*. Translated by Hillel Halkin. Boston: Houghton Mifflin Harcourt, 2006.

Yosef, Raz. "Spectacles of Pain: War, Masculinity and the Masochistic Fantasy in Amos Gitai's 'Kippur'." *Shofar* 24, no. 1 (2005): 49–66. www.jstor.com/stable/42944120.

Zeffren, Ilana. *Pink Story*. Tel Aviv: Mapa, 2005.

Zeffren, Ilana. *Rishumon*. Haifa: Pardes, 2014.

Zeffren, Ilana. "Top Secret." In *Drawing Power: Women's Stories of Sexual Violence, Harassment, and Survival*, edited by Diane Noomin, 178–180. New York: Abrams ComicArts, 2019.

Zeffren, Ilana. "Holidays." http://ilanazeffren.com/Images/moadim-4.jpg.

Zeffren, Ilana. "Zina." http://ilanazeffren.com/Images/Zina-4.jpg.

Zeitlin, Froma I. "The Vicarious Witness: Belated Memory and Authorial Presence in Recent Holocaust Literature." *History and Memory* 10, no. 2 (1998): 5–42. www.jstor.org/stable/25681026.

Index

For Product Safety Concerns and Information please contact our EU
representative GPSR@taylorandfrancis.com
Taylor & Francis Verlag GmbH, Kaufingerstraße 24, 80331 München, Germany

www.ingramcontent.com/pod-product-compliance
Lightning Source LLC
Chambersburg PA
CBHW071054280326
41928CB00050B/2506